MW01015421

# Faith Raising

# vs.

# Money Raising

## An Approach to Doing Stewardship God's Way

Written by

**George O. McCalep, Jr., Ph.D.**

Foreword by

**Dr. Julius Scruggs**

**Vice President**

**National Baptist Convention USA, Inc.**

# Faith Raising vs. Money Raising

Unless otherwise indicated, all scripture quotations are taken from the *Holy Bible, King James Version*.

Faith Raising vs. Money Raising
Copyright © 2003 by Orman Press, Inc.
4200 Sandy Lake Drive, Lithonia, GA  30038

ISBN: 1-891773-40-2

Printed in the United States of America

# Table of Contents

## Part Three:
## Capital Stewardship

## Part Four:
## The McCalep Group

## Epilogue

# Study Guide and Teaching Aid

# About the Author

Dr. George O. McCalep, Jr., has pastored the Greenforest Community Baptist Church in Decatur, Georgia since 1979. Under his leadership over the past twenty-three years, the congregation has grown from 25 members to over 6,000 members, with an average Sunday School attendance of approximately 1,500. The Greenforest ministry includes a $12 million facility that sits on 115 acres, and has a monthly payroll of $500,000. Dr. McCalep founded the Greenforest/McCalep Early Learning Center (ages six months–four years) and Academic Center (grades K–12), that currently have a combined enrollment of 860 students. The Academic Center is fully accredited and was recognized by the Institute for Independent Education in 1994 as "School of the Year." In August 2001, Greenforest constructed a new $8 million state-of-the-art Early Learning Center facility that can house 460 children.

In 1997, Dr. McCalep formed the Greenforest Web Association, an independent, nonprofit corporation that provides networking opportunities, solutions and training to developing ministry-driven, teaching-oriented churches. The Web Association shares a nontraditional model that is accessed through telecommunications, publications, regional workshops and a national Ministry Fest, held annually at Greenforest.

Additionally, Dr. McCalep has led the church in a ministry of economic development that includes the Greenforest Community Development Corporation, a credit union, employment services, social services and a $6 million apartment complex named "The Forest at Columbia."

Dr. McCalep is a retired Georgia State University professor and serves as an adjunct professor at Luther Rice Seminary in Atlanta, teaching Church Growth and Evangelism. He is the author of several notable books. (See "The Author's Collection" at the end of this book.) Most recently, he compiled and edited *Fulfillment Hour,* a nontraditional Sunday School model for every church and denomination.

# Foreword

Dr. McCalep's book *Faith Raising vs. Money Raising: An Approach to Doing Stewardship God's Way* is biblically based and takes the teaching of stewardship to the next dimension. The underlying thesis is that good stewardship is based on faith, love and trust in God rather than on money. It is easy reading, although convicting, in that Dr. McCalep continuously reminds the reader that the Bible states that *"it is impossible to please God without faith"* (Heb. 11:6) and tithing is a matter of faith, not a matter of money.

The book is full of creative illustrations that lead readers into a higher spiritual relationship with God through faithful, obedient use of their gifts, talents, time and money. The sub-headings in the first section of the book are reminiscent of devotional themes that could serve well for quiet time and meditation as well as excellent preaching material. The study guide and detailed appendix only add to the book's user friendliness and resourcefulness.

A book of this magnitude is long overdue. It is one of the rare books on the market that offers a prescribed plan for implementing stewardship in the church. Dr. McCalep's "God's Progressive Giving Plan" is a prototype that when implemented promises any church an increase in giving and a spiritual revival. Additionally, the section on capital fund-raising is based on experience, savvy and a proven success record.

The Epilogue entitled, "Discovering the Joy of Giving" is well worth the price of the book alone. I sincerely believe that *Faith Raising vs. Money Raising* will live up to its claim of bringing about a spiritual awakening, if the concepts are studied, taught, preached and implemented. I have practiced these stewardship principles in the church where I pastor, so I can testify to their benefits. Also, Dr. McCalep's ministry at the Greenforest Community Baptist Church adds volumes of credibility to the book.

Therefore, I recommend this book without hesitation to all individuals and churches.

Dr. Julius Scruggs, Vice President
National Baptist Convention USA, Inc.

# Introduction

Effective stewardship is about faith raising rather than money raising. The emphasis of stewardship should be to increase people's faith rather than raising money. When faith increases, monetary contributions will also increase. *Faith Raising vs. Money Raising* is about doing stewardship God's way. The central message addresses the questions:

> *Effective stewardship is about faith raising rather than money raising.*

- What does God say about money and giving?
- How do you turn the gloomy time of raising the church's annual budget or money for a building project into a time of spiritual awakening?
- How do you transform the congregation to a status of effective stewardship?

## The Undergirding Propositions

Nine basic propositions undergird *Faith Raising vs. Money Raising*. They are:

1. Tithing is a faith matter rather than a money matter, and is critical to our relationship with God.

2. Giving is a measure of our love and gratitude for God.

3. Knowledge of what the Bible says about giving is critical to effective stewardship.

4. Tithes and offerings are God's way of supporting the church.

5. Anointed preaching is the best tool for stewardship transformation.

6. The joy of giving is the ultimate stewardship experience.

7. Full disclosure creates the best environment to teach and implement stewardship God's way.

8. An intentional and planned procedure must be followed to have an effective stewardship program.

9. A separate, intentional procedure should be followed using an outside consultant to be effective in the stewardship of capital campaigns, e.g., building funds.

## Proposition One:
## Tithing is a matter of faith and critical to our relationship with God.

Contrary to popular thinking, tithing is not a money matter. It is an issue of faith. God said, "Try me." or "Prove me."

> *"Bring ye all the tithes into the storehouse, that there may be meat in mine house, and prove me now herewith, saith the* LORD *of hosts, if I will not open you the windows of heaven, and pour you out a blessing, that there shall not be room enough to receive it" (Mal. 3:10).*

This is an invitation to put your faith in God. God wants us dependent on Him. To become like a little child is the challenge. God invites us to demonstrate our faith in Him by giving Him the first 10 percent of what He has allowed us to earn. The teaching of dependence on God stands contrary to the teaching of today's culture that espouses independence and rugged individualism. Likewise, faith stands in opposition to reason and logic. Notice the biblical definition of faith defies the notion that faith can be logical, predictable and reasonable.

*"Now faith is the substance of things hoped for, the evidence of things not seen" (Heb. 11:1).*

If you can see it, it is not faith. If you can logically predict a rational outcome, it is not faith. Therefore, you may not understand how the benefits and results of tithing are possible. Tithing is trusting God to take care of you. Tithing is putting faith in God to supply your needs. The Bible declares that a good steward is found faithful and that it is impossible to please God without faith.

*"Moreover it is required in stewards, that a man be found faithful" (1 Cor. 4:2).*

*"But without faith it is impossible to please him" (Heb. 11:6).*

Therefore, failure to tithe puts us in an imperfect relationship with God. **Tithing is critical to our relationship with God.**

## Proposition Two:
### Giving is a measure of our love and gratitude.

God says in Luke 12:34, *"For where your treasure is, there will your heart be also."* Apparently, offering time is the only time we tell the truth about our love for God and our gratitude to Him. What we give is a eulogistic remark toward God. The ledger sheet or memo in our checkbook mirrors our love for God. Likewise, our church budget reflects what we value most. Churches that value and love youth,

*Loving is reflected in giving.*

budget for youth ministry. Churches that love and value the pastoral leadership honor their pastor in his compensation package. Loving is reflected in giving. The first Commandment tells us to love God with all our heart, mind and soul (Matt. 22:37). Failure to give generously is an act of rebellion against the greatest Commandment. Examining our giving is like putting a thermometer in our mouths to determine the degree of our love for God. *Faith Raising vs. Money Raising* challenges believers to become better stewards based on their thankfulness and love for Christ.

### Proposition Three:
### Knowledge of what the Bible teaches about giving is critical to effective stewardship.

*"My people are destroyed from lack of knowledge" (Hosea 4:6).* The church I have been blessed to pastor has experienced a growth in actual income from $13 thousand to $5 million exclu-

sively in tithes and offerings during a span of twenty-three years. What is the primary cause of the tremendous growth in tithes and

> Faith raising, not money raising is rooted in the biblical principal of giving.

offerings? Knowledge of what the Bible says from cover to cover is the primary reason. Faith raising, not money raising is rooted in the biblical principal of giving. Four biblically based principles are prevalent throughout this book. They are:

1. **Firstfruit giving.** Put God first in your financial priorities. Proverbs 3:9 says, *"Honour the LORD with thy substance, and with the firstfruits of all thine increase."* Matthew 6:33 says, *"Seek ye first the kingdom of God and his righteousness; and all these things shall be added unto you."* On the first day of the week write your first check to the body of Christ (the church).

2. **Purposeful giving.** Purposeful giving is planned giving. Second Corinthians 9:7 says, *"Every man according as he purposeth in his heart, so let him give."* Plan what you will give and when. It should not be a spontaneous act that is not given thought until the offering tray is passed. Also,

plan to grow in your giving. The tithe is the minimum that God requires. It is not the maximum He will accept. Establish giving goals and make them known to those who hold you accountable. Remember a goal untold is a defeatist attitude and a grasshopper perspective. Commitment is necessary for purposeful giving.

3. **Willful giving.** Give willingly with the right motive and attitude. Failure to do this means your efforts are as "hay and stubble" (1 Cor. 3:12) and are all for naught (nothing). *"God loveth a cheerful giver"* (2 Cor. 9:7).

4. **Sacrificial giving.**

   *"And he called unto him his disciples, and saith unto them, Verily I say unto you, That this poor widow hath cast more in than all they which have cast into the treasury: For all they did cast in of their abundance; but she of her want did cast in all that she had, even all her living"* (Mark 12:43,44).

Christian giving is not giving one's fair share." Christian giving is responding to the world's needs as God lets us see them. Those needs require sacrificial giving. Sacrificial giving promotes equal sacrifice, not equal giving.

## Proposition Four:
## Tithes and offerings are God's way of
## · supporting the church.

Selling products and goods is not supported in scripture as a way of funding the church. As a matter of fact, one of Jesus'

> *Selling products and goods is not supported in scripture as a way of funding the church.*

greatest displays of total disgust was when He chased the moneychangers out of the church.

> *"And they come to Jerusalem: and Jesus went into the temple, and began to cast out them that sold and bought in the temple, and overthrew the tables of the moneychangers, and the seats of them that sold doves" (Mark 11:15).*

**Selling raises money. Tithing raises faith. Tithing is God's way.** It is fair and merciful. It represents our faith. It is a thermometer that measures our faith, love and thankfulness.

Many Christians refuse to put this thermometer under their tongues. The key is that each Christian should demonstrate his or her faith according to his or her ability, blessings, mind and heart, empowered by the Holy Spirit.

## Proposition Five: Anointed preaching is the best tool for stewardship transformation.

Anointed preaching is the best tool for stewardship transformation. The stewardship of money must be preached through an anointed vessel on Sunday mornings. The preached word is the best tool for transformation in the church. God has given us an arsenal of tools to change hearts, minds and lives, but none are as effective as the uncompromised, preached word. Workshops, symposiums and Sunday School lessons are good and should be utilized, but nothing can replace the power of the pulpit. Preaching about money is not popular. Therefore, many pastors have sought other ways of teaching about the stewardship of money. Other avenues may be used, but to abandon preaching on what God says about money is a

> *The stewardship of money must be preached through an anointed vessel on Sunday mornings.*

mistake. It is worth noting that the preaching must come through a vessel that has been prepared to preach on giving. If the pastor is not a tither and has not been set free from materialism and other agents of bondage, then your efforts will be ineffective.

November is "Stewardship Emphasis Month" at my church. Every week in November for twenty-three years I have preached a stewardship revival during the prime time Sunday morning worship from the simple theme "What the Bible Says About Giving." The messages have not always been popular, but they have been fruitful.

Our growth in giving has been phenomenal. Nearly two thousand families have committed in writing to grow in their giving as well as tithe. Many give over and above the 10 percent tithe. However, the greatest benefit that has resulted from preaching with convic-tion on money has been the increase in

*Stewardship revival has proven to be more of a spiritual awakening than our traditional summer revival.*

the spirituality of the church and our participating members. Over the past twenty-three years the November stewardship revival has proven to be more of a spiritual awakening than our traditional summer revival.

Tithing increases our faith walk with God. Our relationship with God is determined by our faith and trust in God. No other Christian discipline does as much to assure our relationship with God as tithing. Tithing is integrally related to loving God. Tithing and worshipping God are directly connected. Stewardship is an outgrowth of our discipleship. If a believer is a disciplined disciple, his giving will be in accordance with the Word of God. This is best accomplished through preaching.

*"How then shall they call on him in whom they have not believed? and how shall they believe in him of whom they have not heard? and how shall they hear without a preacher?" (Rom.10:14).*

## Proposition Six:
## The joy of giving is the ultimate stewardship experience.

There is a popular theme in the new millennium church vernacular that is referred to, as the "next level." Is there a next level in stewardship? The answer is "Yes!" The next level in the quest to become good stewards is to discover the joy of giving. Discovering the joy of giving goes beyond giving tithes and offerings.

It is without a doubt the ultimate stewardship experience and it is more than a one-time experience. The joy of giving is a lifestyle

> *The joy of giving is a lifestyle that is motivated by a desire to advance God's kingdom by giving back that which he continues to give you.*

that is motivated by a desire to advance God's kingdom by giving back that which he continues to give you. It is liberating, exciting and joyful. It is a reason for waking up in the morning. It really cannot be explained. It can be described, but it cannot be explained. It must be discovered and experienced.

How do you discover it? You must first want to find it. Like any other treasure, you must look for it. You can look for it in prayer and in the Word of God. To help you find this joyful lifestyle, this book contains an Epilogue entitled, "Discovering the Joy of Giving." Read, meditate, pray and study the series of messages in this section and you will discover the ultimate stewardship experience of the joy of giving.

## Proposition Seven:
## Full disclosure creates the best environment to teach and implement stewardship God's way.

Full disclosure of all money received and spent helps to elimi-nate negative perceptions. Negative perceptions produce an environment that hinders giving. For example, giving is stifled if it is perceived that the pastor or the church is mishandling money. All procedures should be fully disclosed and published in an attempt to alleviate any negative perceptions that would hinder the potential for giving. Church members find it difficult to concentrate on obedient stewardship in a distrustful environment. The church should do everything possible to replace negative perceptions with positive ones. Adopt a full disclosure policy and implement a procedure for regular reporting of all money received and spent.

> *Church members find it difficult to concentrate on obedient stewardship in a distrustful environment.*

## Proposition Eight:
## An intentional, planned procedure must be followed to have an effective stewardship program.

This book gives you all of the information, procedural steps and materials needed to implement an effective stewardship program. The proven prototype is entitled, "God's Progressive Giving Plan." It is an outgrowth of a plan I was introduced to by the Annuity Board of the Southern Baptist Convention twenty-three years ago called the "Forward Plan." God's Progressive Giving

Plan has been implemented at the church where I pastor under various names for the last twenty-three years. It is said that the proof of the pudding is in the eating. Likewise, the proof of a stewardship plan is in the results. This plan has led our congregation from $13 thousand to over $5 million in annual contributions.

Yes, there are other stewardship plans, but I recommend "God's Progressive Giving Plan" without hesitation. It bears my experience and is the essence of my stewardship journey. As

*The proof of a stewardship plan is in the results.*

with any plan, some tweaking will be necessary to fit it to your congregation, but for the most part, it should be followed religiously to guarantee success. Part Two of this book gives a detailed explanation of God's Progressive Giving Plan and step-by-step procedures on implementing the plan.

## Proposition Nine:
## A separate, intentional procedure should be followed using an outside consultant to be effective in the stewardship of capital campaigns.

Capital campaigns are used to financially prepare for building projects. They involve contributions that are separate and over and above the monies collected from tithes and offerings. Tithes and offerings are for the general operating budget. Therefore, a distinctly separate procedure needs to be implemented to raise capital funds. The concept remains the same, raise the spiritual level of the church and you will raise the monies committed and given to special projects.

In my opinion, an outside consultant will greatly contribute to the overall effectiveness of any capital campaign. In general, leaders can be categorized in three groups: (1) "I" leaders; (2) "We" leaders, and (3) "They" leaders. "I" leaders are autocratic dictators. "We" leaders are democratic leaders. "They" leaders are outsiders who bring proven expertise in the areas of need. Even if the "I" leader has as much expertise as the "They" leader, the congregation will usually hold the "They" leader and what he says in higher esteem as an expert. As a matter of fact, my definition of an expert is a well-dressed person from another city (particularly a big city) with a briefcase and a laptop. Seemingly, the bigger the city and the more distance that they have to travel, the greater their credibility.

However, more important than the psychological dynamics is the fact that outside consultants have developed expertise from experience. Experience has always been the best teacher. It could be said like father knows best, consultants know best. I recall the first time I used an outside consultant for a capital campaign. The consultant told me that if I wanted the campaign to fail, then let the current leadership spearhead the campaign.

*Using an outside consultant eliminates the problem of having to overcome what I call "homemade" (unbiblical) fund-raising ideas.*

In other words, if I wanted the campaign to be successful, do not use the current leadership of the church. This simply did not make sense to me. He was right and I am glad I took his advice. Also, using an outside consultant eliminates the problem of having to overcome what I call "homemade" (unbiblical) fund-raising ideas, e.g., assessing each member a predetermined amount of money.

As pastor, I have successfully implemented two capital campaigns. In the first, 450 families raised $1.3 million. In the second, 1,100 families committed to $10 million. The second is still underway and will culminate in 2005. My experience and the lessons learned from these campaigns have led me to organize a stewardship consultant group called "The McCalep Group." This book will introduce you to The McCalep Group; however, due to the extensive nature of a capital campaign, a separate volume of materials has been developed and will be at your disposal if you choose to use The McCalep Group as your capital campaign consultants.

## About This Book

All of the messages in *Faith Raising vs. Money Raising* are purposed to transform congregations to a status of effective, biblical stewardship.

**Part One** offers inspirational messages around what the Bible says about giving and our relationship with God (propositions one through five).

**Part Two** describes God's Progressive Giving Plan and provides implementation instructions.

**Part Three** provides insight into capital campaigns, the factors that influence their success, considerations, cautions and advice on selecting and working with an outside consultant. Several inspirational messages are also included.

**Part Four** introduces the McCalep Group—who we are, our services and the benefits you will derive when selecting us as your capital campaign consultants.

**The Epilogue** contains a six-part series of sermons on how believers can discover the joy of giving. After internalizing and practicing for over twenty-three years all that God has said in His Word about giving, I have discovered the joy of giving. It is a level to which, I believe, every Christian should strive to graduate. It is a place in life and in your relationship with God where you seek opportunities to give for the pure joy of pleasing God and building His kingdom.

**The Study Guide and Teaching Aid** is provided for individual and group study of the principles presented throughout the book. Four separate lessons are included on the following topics:

Lesson One: What the Bible Says About Giving

Lesson Two: God's Progressive Giving Plan

Lesson Three: Capital Stewardship

Lesson Four: Discovering the Joy of Giving

**The Appendix** includes resources and sample materials to support the implementation of God's Progressive Giving Plan.

*Faith Raising vs. Money Raising* is a stewardship and discipleship book that is designed for individual and group study. It will prove beneficial as a required text in any discipleship curriculum. Read it, study it, preach it, implement the procedures and experience an increase in your faith and a stronger relationship with God.

# Part One:

# God's Stewardship Principles

**Proverbs 3:5–10**

$^5$Trust in the LORD with all thine heart; and lean not unto thine own under-standing. $^6$In all thy ways acknowledge him, and he shall direct thy paths. $^7$Be not wise in thine own eyes: fear the LORD, and depart from evil. $^8$It shall be health to thy navel, and marrow to thy bones. $^9$Honour the LORD with thy substance, and with the firstfruits of all thine increase: $^{10}$So shall thy barns be filled with plenty, and thy presses shall burst out with new wine.

**Matthew 16:13–18**

$^{13}$When Jesus came into the coasts of Caesarea Philippi, he asked his disciples, saying, Whom do men say that I the Son of man am? $^{14}$And they said, Some *say that thou art* John the Baptist: some, Elias; and others, Jeremias, or one of the prophets. $^{15}$He saith unto them, But whom say ye that I am? $^{16}$And Simon Peter answered and said, Thou art the Christ, the Son of the living God. $^{17}$And Jesus answered and said unto him, Blessed art thou, Simon Bar-jona: for flesh and blood hath not revealed *it* unto thee, but my Father which is in heaven. $^{18}$And I say also unto thee, That thou art Peter, and upon this rock I will build my church; and the gates of hell shall not prevail against it.

# Acknowledge God

Although Proverbs is considered a Hebrew book of poetry, it is still the authoritative word and truth of God. We often compare similarities and differences of Proverbs with the book of Psalms. Both are poetic; however, the book of Psalms is of poetic expressions of praise. In contrast, the book of Proverbs is a book of wisdom, i.e. wise sayings. King Solomon prayed for wisdom (1 Kings 3:5–9). God gave him wisdom and riches.

If we had one prayer today, would it be for wisdom? I am afraid that many of us would not pray for wisdom. Many of us would pray for something material. Many of us think that we need a new car, house, husband or wife. I've a feeling that if we had one prayer, very few of us would pray like King Solomon prayed and ask for wisdom. As a matter of fact, many of us act like we don't really want to know anything. When we hear tithing testimonies our actions say, "I don't want to hear about committing to tithing." Our attendance in Bible Study and Fulfillment Hour (Sunday School) and the dust collecting on some of our Bibles indicate that we don't want to know any-thing. We don't want to know nothing or nut'n'. We're like the commercial on TV for Nut 'n' Honey.

> *When we first acknowledge God, we eliminate the "Nut 'n', Honey" attitude.*

What is our testimony for the Lord? Nut 'n', Honey. What have we done for Him lately? Nut 'n', Honey. We need to discard the "Nut 'n', Honey" attitude. The antidote for the poisoning of a "Nut 'n', Honey" attitude is to acknowledge God. When we first acknowledge God, we eliminate the "Nut 'n', Honey" attitude.

## Do You Really Know God?

At Caesarea Philippi, Jesus asked the disciples, *"Whom do men say that I the Son of man am?" (Matt.16:13)*. They had many responses. Some said John the Baptist, some Jeremias. Others said Elijah. After all, He was supposed to come back. Then Jesus put the question more pointedly, *"But whom say ye that I am?*

*And Simon Peter said, Thou art the Christ, the Son of the living God" (Matt 16:15,16).* Jesus said, *"[Peter], for flesh and blood hath not revealed it unto thee, but my Father which is in heaven…Upon this rock I will build my church" (Matt. 16:17-18).* Jesus was saying, upon this acknowledgement I will build my church. It all begins with the acknowledgement of God. The word, acknowledge, comes from two Greek words—epi and ginosko. Epi means "upon." Ginosko means "to know." Together, epiginosko means "upon knowing." It carries a deeper connotation than our "to know" because it carries an "exactness"—*to recognize and know exactly, to confirm and affirm.* The indication from the grammar is that it requires a response to make the sentence complete. Upon knowing what? Something has to come after "upon knowing." Upon knowing Him, we will love Him. Upon knowing Him, we will serve Him. Upon knowing Him, we will confess Him. Upon knowing Him, we will accept Him. Upon knowing Him, we will give to Him. If we really know God, then we will acknowledge Him.

> Something has to come after "upon knowing." Upon knowing Him, we will love Him.

## Lean Not to Your Own Understanding

*"Trust in the LORD with all thine heart… In all thy ways acknowledge Him and He shall direct thy paths" (Prov. 3:5,6).* To know Him is to trust Him and to lean not on your own understanding. Some of us are leaning on our own understanding. My most fervent prayer is that the church comes under submission to the authoritative Word of God. Then we will become issue-free. There can be no issue if the church is under submission to the authoritative Word of God. We won't have any issues as a church or as individuals.

Too many of us are leaning on our own understanding. Where did we get it? Some of us got it from our mothers, fathers, grandmothers, or grandfathers. Some of us got it from the schools we've attended and the places we've worked. We've gotten it from a lot of places. I am not saying that you should not think. God gave you a conscious mind. He did that for higher animals. Lower animals have an unconscious instinct. They do not have a conscious mind like we do. How is it that God would be mindful of man to give us a consciousness? Your conscience is the mind of your soul, but your conscience can go awry. The conscience can become corrupt. However God has given you His word and the ability to pray and meditate so you do not have to lean to your own understanding. To know God is to lean not on your own understanding. To know God is to acknowledge Him and let Him direct your path. The Psalmist says, *"Thy word is a lamp unto my feet and a light unto my path" (Psalm 119:105).*

## Firstfruit Giving

If we know God, we will give Him the firstfruits of our substance. On your entries in your checkbook, what number was your entry for God? That may be a somewhat sobering question for many of us. All of us pay bills. Most of us use checking accounts. Over the years, God's grace has allowed me to make the first entry to Greenforest Baptist Church. We have to do it first.

> To know God is to acknowledge Him and let Him direct your path.

Tithing is not a money matter. It is a faith matter. God's Progressive Giving Plan moves us toward the ultimate tithe. God approves that. If our faith is not at the 10 percent tithe, then we are to give at the level where we are with it purposed in our hearts to grow to the tithe. Less than 10 percent is not the tithe, but God will bless your efforts if it is done according to

His biblical principles. If we have the faith to make the ultimate leap to 10 percent, if we have the faith of a mustard seed and want to expand it, then we are to work with that much faith. God approves, but we have to do it first. Too many of our checkbook entries are to everybody else.

Let's write our bills out right now. I believe the first bill we pay is the mortgage. Next we pay the utility bill. Then, we pay the car note. Who do we pay next? Groceries, insurance, Dillard's, Rich's-Macy's, J.C. Penney, Sears, MasterCard, Visa, Diner's Club, American Express, American Express Gold and American Express Platinum. We've written a whole lot of bills. Where is God? We know where He's supposed to be, don't we? Somewhere down the line, we have an entry to God that is probably too little.

> *You and God together can do more with 90 percent than you can do with 100 percent alone.*

Try God's way and see if He won't open the windows of heaven and pour out a blessing for you. I am a tither. My congregation has watched my wife and me grow in our giving. Every year I tell them the percentage of our income that we give to the church. I don't ask anybody else to do that, but I want the congregation to know what their pastor does. I'm not bragging.

As their leader, I want them to know that my wife and I have grown from 10 to 21 percent and we give it first! You and God together can do more with 90 percent than you can do with 100 percent alone. Upon knowing God, you can trust Him. Upon knowing God, you can give Him the firstfruits.

## A Divine Audit

Do you know that there will be a divine audit one day? If you think it's scary to go before the Internal Revenue Service, wait until you have to account for what you've done with what God has given you. I can hear some of us saying, "I had to pay my bills. I couldn't afford it." The rich man is going to have a divine audit and so will the poor man. The one who has only one talent is going to have a divine audit *There will be a divine audit one day.* just like the one who had five. God will want to know what you did with that one talent that he gave you. God will want to know what you did with your paycheck and your worker's compensation check. God will want to know what you did with your unemployment check. God will want to know what you did with your welfare check. It all comes from Him. All good and perfect things come from the Lord (James 1:17a). Will you pass the audit?

## Summary

The ultimate question is the one that the disciples were given at Caesarea Philippi when Jesus asked them, "Who do men say that I am?" (Matt. 16:13b). They began to battle around. I think in our minds some of us are battling around. We think Jesus is somebody that a whole lot of people come to church to talk about on Sunday morning. After they battled it around, He asked the question of Peter and He's asking us, "Don't worry about who men say that I am. Don't worry about popular opinion. Who do you say I am?" Peter said, "You are the Christ, the son of the living God" (Matt. 16:16b). Jesus told Peter, "Flesh and blood did not reveal that, but my Father in heaven. And thou art Peter" (Matt. 16:17b, 18a). When Peter acknowledged Jesus, Jesus acknowledged Him.

When we acknowledge God, God will acknowledge us. He said, *"Upon this rock [upon you], I will build my church"* (Matt. 16:18). Acknowledge Him and everything else will grow out of Him.

**Malachi 3:8–18 (NIV)**

[8]"Will a man rob God? Yet you rob me. "But you ask, 'How do we rob you?' "In tithes and offerings. [9]You are under a curse-the whole nation of you because you are robbing me. [10]Bring the whole tithe into the storehouse, that there may be food in my house. Test me in this," says the LORD Almighty, "and see if I will not throw open the floodgates of heaven and pour out so much blessing that you will not have room enough for it. [11]I will prevent pests from devouring your crops, and the vines in your fields will not cast their fruit," says the LORD Almighty. [12]"Then all the nations will call you blessed, for yours will be a delightful land," says the LORD Almighty. [13]"You have said harsh things against me," says the LORD. "Yet you ask, 'What have we said against you?' [14]"You have said, 'It is futile to serve God. What did we gain by carrying out his requirements and going about like mourners before the LORD Almighty? [15]But now we call the arrogant blessed. Certainly the evildoers prosper, and even those who challenge God escape.'"[16]Then those who feared the LORD talked with each other, and the LORD listened and heard. A scroll of remembrance was written in his presence concerning those who feared the LORD and honored his name. [17]"They will be mine," says the LORD Almighty, "in the day when I make up my treasured possession. I will spare them, just as in compassion a man spares his son who serves him. [18]And you will again see the distinction between the righteous and the wicked, between those who serve God and those who do not.

# The Biblical Principle of the Tithe:

## God's Standard for Giving

What is a standard? A standard is an acknowledged comparison of value. It is a degree or level of requirement for attainment. A standard is a measure of value. A standard is an average, but acceptable quality. What is a principle? A principle is a rule or a standard. A principle is a fixed, predetermined policy or mode of action. A principle is a rule or law concerning the functioning of natural or spiritual phenomena.

## God's Standard for Giving

Christians should follow the biblical principle of the tithe as God's standard for giving. Standards are not foreign to us. We gauge life's values by standards. There are standard athletic fields, e.g., baseball diamonds and football fields. A football field is 50 yards long. It is not 45 yards long on one side and 50 yards on the other. If you play on a field like that, it is not qualified. The baseball used in the major leagues is a standard baseball. Barry Bonds hit 73 home runs in one season using standard baseballs. If one ball had been proclaimed to be less than standard, he would have only had 72 home runs. The baseballs had to meet the standard.

We gauge our time based on standards, e.g., Eastern Standard Time. There is a standard of living. (I find it very interesting that we don't like to live below the standard of living, yet we will give below the standard of giving.) There is a standard body temperature of 98.6 degrees. When we go to the doctor and he or she puts the thermometer in our mouth, if it doesn't register according to the standard, the doctor declares us to be sick.

> *We can tip the person who brings the food to the table, but we can't tithe to the one who put the food on the table.*

There is also a standard tip. It was once 10 percent. They bring us the bill and we just sign it and put 10 percent on it. Something is wrong when we can tip the person who brings the food to the table, but we can't tithe to the one who put the food on the table. God made the food. He gave us the breath to eat it. He gave us a digestive system, and yet we can tip a man or woman, but can't tithe to God.

It is interesting that the standard tip has now gone up. It's not 10 percent anymore, it's 15 percent. And if you have six or more in your party, the tip will be 18 percent. If you have a party of 10 they don't even ask how thankful you are for the service. They put a gratuity on the bill of 21 percent. They just add it on. Now look at how good God is. He has never raised His standard. We ought to be excited that God, throughout existence before the law, after the law, and during the law, never raised His standard. What if God were to raise His standard from 10 percent to 50 percent? What if God, like man, decided that He would not ask for a tithe anymore but would just take it? God is a good God.

## Standard Deviation

The problem we have is that we have deviated from the standard. I remember when I took statistics at the University of Kansas, I learned of a unit of measurement called the standard deviation. It would determine how far away you are from the norm or from the standard. When we give less than a dime out of every dollar, we have gone far away from the standard. We deviate from the standard when we give less than a penny out of every dime. God only asks for a penny out of every dime.

We have not only deviated in our giving, but we have also deviated in our moral and ethical living and behavior. We call it alternative lifestyles. When we shack up rather than engage in

*We have deviated so far from God's standard that we can see an arrogant person and call that person blessed.*

holy marriage, we have not chosen an alternative, we have deviated. When men go to bed with men, and women go to bed with women, it is not an alternative, it is a deviation. We dress up sin so it will look good and we call sin an alternative, but it is not an alternative, it is a deviation.

This is what Malachi 3:14 (NIV) says about our deviation: *"You have said, 'It is futile to serve God. What did we gain by carrying out his requirements [standards]...?'"* Malachi goes on to say, *"We call the arrogant blessed."* We have deviated so far from God's standard that we can see an arrogant person and call that person blessed. In verses 17–18 (NIV), God says:

*"They will be mine," says the LORD Almighty, "in the day when I make up my treasured possession. I will spare them, just as in compassion a man spares his son who serves him. And you*

*will again see the distinction between the righteous and the wicked, between those who serve God and those who do not."*

There is going to come a day when the wicked shall be judged, and those who serve God. We will know who is arrogant, who is blessed and who is not blessed.

## A Measure of Worship

The standard of the tithe is a measure of our worship. We worship Him in spirit and in truth. The tithe assures us that we worship Him in truth. We may praise Him with our hands, dance and singing. We also must praise Him in truth. If we are not tithing we are not worshiping in truth. How awful it would be to usher ourselves behind the throne into the very presence of the living God and have Him refuse our praise because we are worshiping Him only in spirit and not in truth.

*The standard of the tithe is a measure of our worship.*

## A Measure of Love

**The standard of the tithe is the measure of the sincerity of our love.** If we love Him we will serve Him, obey His principles and meet His standard. Our "Prove the Tithe Sunday" could be called "Prove Your Love Sunday" because it is a time to demonstrate our sincere love for God.

## A Measure of Faith

The standard of the tithe is a measure of our faith in Him. Tithing is not a money matter. It is a faith matter. The question

*The standard of the tithe is a measure of our faith in Him.*

is, Do you have enough faith to believe that God will take care of you? God says, "Prove me, test me, try me, herewith. If you give me my tithe, then I will take care of you. Not only will I take care of you, but I will open up the floodgates of heaven and pour you out a blessing that you will not have room to hold" (Mal. 3:10b).

It is not a question of money. It is a question of faith. Faith is very important. Faith is critical. We are saved by grace through faith. The Bible tells us that it is impossible to please God without faith. Do you want to please Him? If so, you have to have faith. We are saved by His grace and by the faith that He has given us. So all of us can do some percentage. You may not have a measure of 10 or a measure of 20, but you do have a measure of faith.

## A Measure of Gratitude

The tithe is the standard by which we measure the sincerity of our gratitude. How thankful are we? What kind of gratuity are we going to put on the altar? We give the waiter 15 percent. What's our gratuity to God? How grateful are we for what He has done for us?

*The tithe is the standard by which we measure the sincerity of our gratitude.*

## Summary

The tithe is a measure of His love for us. God says, of everything that we earn, He will take one and we can have nine. God says give me one dollar, and you take nine dollars. He is a good God! His standard is not only our proof of our love for Him, our believing in Him and our trusting in Him, it is also a measure of His love for us.

**Malachi 3:8–12**

8 Will a man rob God? Yet ye have robbed me. But ye say, Wherein have we robbed thee? In tithes and offerings. 9 Ye *are* cursed with a curse: for ye have robbed me, *even* this whole nation. 10 Bring ye all the tithes into the storehouse, that there may be meat in mine house, and prove me now herewith, saith the LORD of hosts, if I will not open you the windows of heaven, and pour you out a blessing, that *there shall* not *be room* enough *to receive it.* 11 And I will rebuke the devourer for your sakes, and he shall not destroy the fruits of your ground; neither shall your vine cast her fruit before the time in the field, saith the LORD of hosts. 12 And all nations shall call you blessed: for ye shall be a delightsome land, saith the LORD of hosts.

# Would You Steal From Your Parent?

This is a personal message for YOU, not your spouse or someone you know. God is asking you the question, Would you steal from your parent? Psychological and pathological research verifies that when one steals from one's parent, provider or protector, something is wrong. The pathological behavior of a child stealing from his parent is a usually an indication that the child is on drugs or something has gone seriously awry.

We all know that persons addicted to crack cocaine will steal from their daddy, mama, or anybody else. Our prisons are filled with young men and women who are incarcerated for stealing and other crimes that were committed

*Psychological and pathological research verifies that when one steals from one's parent, provider or protector, something is wrong.*

for drugs. They are incarcerated for stealing, but their problem is drugs. They are not really criminals. They are drug addicts.

Something is wrong when one steals from one's parent. Even many lower forms of animals will not steal from their parents or the hands that feeds them. In other words, Baby Bear will not steal from Mama Bear or Papa Bear. Baby Bear might steal the basket out of our van, but Baby Bear won't touch anything that belongs to Mama Bear or Papa Bear. That is why God asks us to consider this serious question: Would a man rob God?

*Something is not right when a believer steals from his or her Father.*

## Would a Man Rob God?

Would a person rob his parent? His maker? His provider? His savior? His redeemer? In Malachi's day, this was the question God put forth to the people. This is the question He is asking us today. We, like the people of old, because of our lack of spiritual development or maybe our naivete, ignorance or rebellious spirit, answer with the question, How have we robbed you, Father? God says we have robbed Him in tithes and offerings. Therefore, He says:

*"Bring me all of the tithes into mine house [not United Way's house or NAACP, as good as they might be, but into mine house] so that there will be meat in mine house, and prove me herewith, and see if I won't open up the windows of heaven and pour you out a blessing that there will not be room enough to receive. And I will rebuke the devourer for your sakes...And all nations shall call you blessed for ye shall be a delightful land [a delightsome church, a delightsome person]"* (Mal. 3:10–12).

Again, the question is, Would a believer rob his parent? Something is not right when a believer steals from his or her Father. Something is not right when we steal from our Daddy. The problem is that we act like we have no God. We act like God is not our Father. We act like we made ourselves. It is bad when we think that we have pulled ourselves up by our own bootstraps. That's stealing God's glory. It is even worse when we think we are successful self-made men. Psalm 100:3 tells us: *"Know ye that the LORD he is God: it is he that hath made us, and not we ourselves."* Yet, we act like God is not our Father. We pray as He has taught us to pray, "Our Father who art in heaven" (Matt. 6:9a), but we act like we are fatherless children.

The Bible tells us in Romans 8:14–15, *"For as many as are led by the Spirit of God, they are the sons of God…ye have received the Spirit of adoption, whereby we cry, Abba, Father."* The word "Abba" means "Daddy." Galatians 4:6–7 says:

> *"And because ye are sons, God hath sent forth the Spirit of his Son into your hearts, crying, Abba, Father. Wherefore thou art no more a servant, but a son; and if a son, then an heir of God through Christ."*

Howbeit that we have known God, and more importantly, as the text says, God has known us, and we are no more servants, but children of God who have been set free, yet we desire to live in bondage?

This is a serious problem. This is a serious sin. This is a serious crime. Would a man steal from God? Would a man take from his provider? God asks us this piercing question because He loves us. The souls of men and women are precious to God. Lives of men and women are precious unto God. Because we are so precious to God, He asks us to ponder this very serious question in our hearts, Would you rob your Daddy? How can you love someone and rob Him at the same time?

## A Serious Crime

Let's look at the seriousness of this crime. Firstly, it is astonishing that this crime could ever be committed. God even puts the question to us as if it were improbable: *"Would a man rob God?" (Mal.3:8)*. It is against even our carnal nature to rob the hand that feeds us. It is unnatural to steal from one who provides for you. Historically, we learn that heathen nations have always built temples for their little "g" gods and brought treasures into these temples for their gods. No heathen would dare rob that temple. Yet, here we are stealing from a living God whom we

*It is against even our carnal nature to rob the hand that feeds us.*

know and who has known us. It is really unbelievable that a man or woman would rob God. It is astonishing, amazing and improbable that one would commit a crime that goes against the very nature of our instincts.

Secondly, it is a serious and terribly shameful crime. In football and basketball, a flagrant foul is a foul that has the potential of injuring someone. In football, you can be penalized five yards for grabbing a player's mask, or 15 yards for holding and jerking the mask. Stealing from your parent is a flagrant foul. It is not a misdemeanor. It is a felony. To rob God is the worst, most

---
*Stealing from your parent is a flagrant foul. It is not a misdemeanor.*

---

naughty, most extravagant crime that could possibly be committed. No words that have been used to describe the evil of September 11, 2001 begin to adequately describe this heinous, excessive, provocative crime of stealing from God. It is a terrible thing to rob your maker.

## A Terrible Crime

Why is stealing from God such a terrible crime? It is terrible because it is done in God's presence. Usually, when we steal something, we do it in the dark. It is deceptive. When we steal, we do it when nobody is looking. We do it on the sly. But when we rob God, we rob Him in His face. We say, "In your face, God!" Also, it is a terrible crime because it injures God's kingdom, God's purpose, God's people, and it injures us.

Because it is such a terrible crime, God punishes it with a terrible punishment. That is why He says, *"Ye are cursed with a curse" (Mal. 3:9).* Our nation is cursed. Our communities are cursed. Our city is cursed. Our church is cursed and we are individually cursed. This terrible crime deserves God's strongest punishment and wrath. A person who robs his creator, parent, friend and savior, commits a serious and terrible crime. Again, I ask this piercing, personal, penetrating to the heart question, Would you steal from your heavenly Father?

## An Ignorant and Stupid Crime

Stealing from God is an ignorant and stupid crime. **It is a stupid crime because we know we will be caught and we know we will be punished.** Why would we commit a crime knowing we will be caught? It is bad to steal, but when we steal knowing we will be caught, that's dumb. We have nowhere to hide. *Because it is such a terrible crime, God punishes it with a terrible punishment.* Osama bin Laden is supposed to be hiding somewhere in a cave. Eric Robert Rudolph is supposed to be hiding somewhere in the mountains of North Carolina. They are America's most wanted criminals and they have places to hide, but when we rob God, the omnipresent, omnipotent one, we have nowhere to hide. That is the ignorance and stupidity of the crime.

It is also stupid because when we rob God, we rob our-selves. We even rob ourselves from God. We take us from God. When we rob God of ourselves, we cut the throat of our own happiness. We steal our own joy and spill poison all over our own blessings. This is the ignorance and stupidity of the crime.

> *It is also stupid because when we rob God, we rob ourselves.*

The Bible tells us in Romans 8:16–17 that the Spirit bears witness with our spirit that we are children of God; and if we are children of God, then we are heirs of God, and joint heirs with Christ. This means that when we rob God, we steal our own inheritance. We injure and curse ourselves. We sign our own death warrant.

## A Solution for the Crime

There is a solution for the crime—to confess and repent. The first part of the solution is confession. We've robbed God of more than just tithes and offerings. We've robbed Him of His praise, worship, time, glory and influence. We need to confess to our heavenly Father that we have been robbing Him. We also need to repent. To repent means that we are not just sorry about it, but we are going to make a complete turn around and stop robbing God. God has asked me to call us into repentance. So in obedience to Almighty God, if you have been robbing God, confess and repent.

There is a provision for our crime. Very simply, God died for our sins and was raised for our justification. Justification means that He has made it right. When we were kids we always tried to justify when we were wrong. We would say to our parents, "I'm not the only one who's guilty." That's trying to justify our behavior. God is the justifier. He will take our faith and justify our wrong, if we confess and repent.

*There is a provision for our crime.*

## Summary

Do you have enough faith to stop robbing God? To stop stealing from your parent? God demonstrated His faithfulness when He died between two thieves, two thieves just like you and me. You need to know that God will forgive you of your robbery. Confess and repent. Stop robbing your parent.

**2 Corinthians 9:6–15**

[6]But this I *say*, He which soweth sparingly shall reap also sparingly; and he which soweth bountifully shall reap also bountifully. [7]Every man according as he purposeth in his heart, *so let him give*; not grudgingly, or of necessity: for God loveth a cheerful giver. [8]And God is able to make all grace abound toward you; that ye, always having all sufficiency in all *things*, may abound to every good work: [9](As it is written, He hath dispersed abroad; he hath given to the poor: his righteousness remaineth for ever. [10]Now he that ministereth seed to the sower both minister bread for *your* food, and multiply your seed sown, and increase the fruits of your righteousness;) [11]Being enriched in every thing to all bountifulness, which causeth through us thanksgiving to God. [12]For the administration of this service not only supplieth the want of the saints, but is abundant also by many thanksgivings unto God; [13]While by the experiment of this ministration they glorify God for your professed subjection unto the gospel of Christ, and for *your* liberal distribution unto them, and unto all *men*; [14]And by their prayer for you, which long after you for the exceeding grace of God in you. [15]Thanks be unto God for his unspeakable gift.

# God's Spiritual Business Plan

As you know, you need a business plan for any business endeavor. As a matter of fact, if you don't have a business plan you will probably fail. People don't plan to fail, they fail to plan. A business plan will describe who you are, your services or product, what you do, and how much you plan or think you are going to do. You project your results based on what you say you are going to do. If you are going to borrow money from a bank for a business, you must have a business plan. You can't go to the bank saying, "I've got an idea. Will you lend me some money?" They will laugh you out of town. You have to present a business plan to the bank, if they are going to loan you some money.

Before the beginning of time, God wrote a spiritual business plan to assure our success. He wrote a spiritual plan based on a spiritual law that guarantees that we will be successful and

*Before the beginning of time, God wrote a spiritual business plan to assure our success.*

blessed. Notice, I said it guarantees success. He wrote a spiritual plan in His eternal Word before the beginning of time that, if we follow it, will guarantee us abundant blessings—not just ordinary blessings, abundant blessings.

## A Spiritual Plan Based on a Spiritual Law

In the Book of 2 Corinthians, Paul writes to the church at Corinth encouraging them to give an offering to the church at Jerusalem. Of course, this message is for us too. Chapters 8 and 9 are all about Christian giving and the grace of giving. All we probably need to know about Christian giving is found in 2 Corinthians 8 and 9.

By the time we get to verse 6 of chapter 9, God is ready to lay out the nuts and bolts of the blessing plan. He begins by telling us in verse 6 that a spiritual law undergirds the plan.

*"He which soweth sparingly shall reap also sparingly; and he which soweth bountifully shall reap also bountifully"*
*(2 Cor. 9:6).*

We have heard this about agriculture and we know it is true. God is using a farming illustration to describe a theological, spiritual law. Now this is God's law. It is an absolute, eternal, guaranteed law. In Genesis 8:22, we read:

*"While the earth remaineth, seedtime and harvest, and cold and heat, and summer and winter, and day and night shall not cease."*

As long as the earth remains, so will the law of seedtime and harvest. Just as sure as the sun comes up and goes down, it shall not cease. This is a spiritual plan based on a spiritual law.

> *As long as the earth remains, so will the law of seedtime and harvest. Just as sure as the sun comes up and goes down, it shall not cease.*

What do I mean when I say based on a spiritual law? An eternal God underwrites a spiritual law. The one who underwrites something puts up the money so that even if nobody shows up, it will still work. God based his business plan on a spiritual law and underwrote it by His own sovereignty. Verse 9 says, "It is written." Whenever we see "it is written," it means that it is non-negotiable and irrevocable. That means God is not going to change His mind. So here we have a plan written before the beginning of time that is non-negotiable, irrevocable, undergirded by a spiritual law and underwritten by God Himself, the Eternal One.

> *God based his business plan on a spiritual law and underwrote it by His own sovereignty.*

## A Plan Administered by Grace

**God's business plan is a covenant that is administered with all grace.** Second Corinthians 9:8 says, *"God is able to make all grace abound toward you."* What a plan! It is covered and implemented with grace and not just grace, but *all grace.* We know that grace is sufficient, but what about *all* grace?

If there is *all* grace, there must be *some* grace that is less than all grace. Dr. A. Louis Patterson, says that there are levels of grace. There is "common grace" that rains on the just and the unjust (Matt. 5:45b). That means God blesses the righteous and the unrighteous. Some of us are living today because of common grace. There is "salvation grace." That is the grace that you received when you accepted Jesus as your Savior. It is by grace that we are saved through faith. There is "living grace" where the things we need to live from day-to-day are blessings from God. If we have a car, a house and a few dollars in the bank, we are quick to tell anybody, "The Lord has blessed me." This is the level where we stop. Most of us never get beyond living grace.

However, there is a level of "all grace." When we have all grace, we live beyond creature comforts. We have joy that the world can't take from us. We have love that will cause us to love our enemies. We have

*There is a level of "all grace."*

peace that surpasses all understanding. There are plenty of people lying in king-size beds who can't sleep at night. There are people wearing expensive shoes who don't have joy in their walk. All grace gives us everlasting peace and joy.

## Plan That Reaches Abroad

There's one more thing you should know—**God's business plan reaches abroad.** Second Corinthians 9:9 says, *"He hath dispersed abroad."* Abroad means it is somewhere other than where I live and not just where I live now, but wherever I live and wherever I go. God's plan is universal. It doesn't matter what business I'm in—computers, teaching or groceries. As long as I'm doing good works, this spiritual plan is guaranteed to reach abroad. In other words, God doesn't want to just bless me at Greenforest Community Baptist Church. Before the beginning of time, in a prenatal era, God wrote a plan to bless me with success wherever I go as long as I'm doing His good works.

He blessed me on the hill of Alabama A&M University when I was a motherless child. He blessed me when I went to the University of Kansas and was the only African American in my class. He blessed me when I went to Ohio State University and drove 140 miles back and forth to Cleveland for a year while working three jobs. He blessed me when I was coaching football in rural Alabama. He blessed me when I was working with the Job Corps in Ohio. He blessed me when I was teaching in the inner city Hough area of Cleveland where there were riots. He blessed me when I was in the investment business in 1973. He has blessed me for twenty-three years now as pastor of Greenforest Community Baptist Church. He's done it all because His plan says that He will bless me abroad. What a plan!

## Tightfisted Seed Consumers

So what's our problem? Why do we not take advantage of God's spiritual business plan? Our problem is that we are "tightfisted seed consumers." Second Corinthians 9:9 says, *"As it is written, He hath dispersed abroad; he hath given to the poor."* That throws us because we don't understand who God is speaking about when He says He has given food to the poor. Who are the poor? The word

> Our problem is that we are "tightfisted seed consumers."

poor in this text means "getting along on meager fair; that is, living from paycheck to paycheck. Does that resemble any of us?

*"Now he that ministereth seed to the sower both minister bread for your food, and multiply your seed sown, and increase the fruits of your righteousness" (2 Cor. 9:10).*

In 2 Corinthians 9:10, we learn that God has given us seed for food and sowing and He plans to multiply that which is sown. However, there is nothing for him to multiply because we consume all the seed on ourselves. We hold on to the seed. God gives us an ear of corn and we eat the whole thing. There is no seed left to sow in good works. In other words, we eat up our abundant blessings.

Eating our abundant blessings is evidence of the fact that what we claim to be a blessing is really sinful selfishness. If all my blessings stop with me, that is selfish. We are tightfisted seed consumers and that is why many of us are just getting along on meager fair. We pass up the opportunity to sow good seeds by eating up all the seeds for ourselves. God has added to our lives, but we're holding it in our fists. We need to open our fists and throw out the seeds. The results will be the same as they

*We eat up our abundant blessings.*

were in Corinth, two thousand years ago. We will demonstrate our obedience and subjection to the gospel, and our love for Christ. It will also unite us in a fellowship of love and thanksgiving.

## Setting Our Own Limitations

**God's spiritual plan allows us to set our own limitations based upon our sowing.** Actually, we set our limitations based on three things—our ambition, attitude and actions.

We find our ambition in 2 Corinthians 9:7, *"As he purposeth in his heart…"* Purpose is our ambition. Our attitude is whether we give grudgingly or cheerfully. God loves a cheerful giver. Many of us can never be blessed because of our attitude. We purpose in our hearts with our ambition, but we give grudgingly out of necessity with an attitude of "I have to" instead of "I want to." Our attitude should be willing and cheerful. Our activity should be "sowing" good works.

Many of us will be crying in heaven because we were tight-fisted seed consumers. Did you think there would be no tears in heaven because God would have wiped them all away? When you get to heaven after having experienced salvation grace and living grace, and you see all the blessings that God had your name on that you could have had while you were on earth, He will have to wipe your tears away because you are going to do some boo-hooing. You won't be weeping. You'll be boo-hooing.

> *God blesses us to be generous, not prosperous. He only wants us to prosper so we can be generous.*

## Generosity Produces Prosperity

God blesses us to be generous, not prosperous. He only wants us to prosper so we can be generous. If we cannot be generous, He does not want us to be prosperous. So the only way we can be prosperous is to be generous, and the only way to do that is to sow good works.

We need to know that God never multiplies what He has added. God adds to the sower's seed. Matthew 6:33 says, *"Seek ye first the kingdom of God and His righteousness; and all these [other] things shall be added unto you."* He has added to our bank accounts. He's added to our houses. He's added to our blessings. He has already added, but multiplication only comes when we sow. He adds, but we have to sow. Then, He will multiply what we sow.

## Summary

God has given us a spiritual business plan that is based on spiritual law. It is an eternal plan that guarantees our success. All we need to do is sow good works generously and cheerfully. A caution here—often we make the mistake of looking for something broken that we can fix. Sometimes that is all right, but we need to understand that when we get ready to sow, we need to look for rich soil. We should look for good soil where God is already blessing. Don't put your seed in bad soil because the birds may come and eat it. The

> *Understand that when we get ready to sow, we need to look for rich soil. We should look for good soil where God is already blessing.*

weeds, rocks and thicket could choke it out. Sow your seeds in good soil and then stand back and watch God work.

**Mark 12:41–44**

41And Jesus sat over against the treasury, and beheld how the people cast money into the treasury: and many that were rich cast in much. 42And there came a certain poor widow, and she threw in two mites, which make a farthing. 43And he called *unto him* his disciples, and saith unto them, Verily I say unto you, That this poor widow hath cast more in, than all they which have cast into the treasury: 44For all *they* did cast in of their abundance; but she of her want did cast in all that she had, even all her living.

# God Watches What You Give to the Church

God watches what you give to the church. Unfortunately, some of us have not spiritualized that truth. It is one thing to know it and hear it, but it is another thing to spiritually understand that every time the offering plate is passed, the almighty living God is watching what you give to the church. Scripture authenticates the fact that God watches what you give to the church.

> Scripture authenticates the fact that God watches what you give to the church.

## Jesus' Last Act of Public Ministry

As we look at Mark 12:41–44, the time is Tuesday of Holy Week and the setting is the Temple in Jerusalem, God's church of biblical time. On Sunday of Holy Week, the Sunday we call Palm Sunday, Jesus rode into Jerusalem on a donkey. On Monday of

Holy Week He taught us one of the most important lessons of the church relative to raising money in the church, He chased the moneychangers out of the Temple. On Tuesday, some forty-eight hours before Jesus was to be crucified on the cross, He chose to sit and watch what people gave to the church. I believe in my heart that there is something significant about this being His last public act of ministry before going to the cross. He deliberately chose to watch what people gave to the church.

Do you believe the scriptural truth that God is the same today as He was yesterday and will be the same tomorrow? If you believe that, then you need to know that if Jesus sat down 2000 years ago and watched what they gave, then you can believe that He is watching what we give today.

## A Lesson in Giving

How did Jesus watch? The Bible says He beheld *(theoreo)*. We get our word "theater" from *theoreo*. When we go to the theater we don't take our eyes off of the screen. As a matter of fact, even if we are eating popcorn, we still don't take our eyes off of the screen. Jesus gazed at the people just like we gaze at the theater screen. He didn't miss a thing. He watched them continually, individually and comprehensively. The Bible says He saw a crowd. He saw many rich people who gave much and He saw one poor widow. He watched continually, deliberately, and with a purpose.

Historians tell us that the treasury was near the Court of Women (where the women had to sit in those days), and the Court of Gentiles (an area for non-Jews). The Bible says He watched a crowd of people. He watched many rich people who gave much. He didn't see anybody stealing. That was not the issue. He didn't say that the rich should not give much. The rich should indeed bring much, but that was not the issue either. He saw the rich, and then He saw a poor widow. She had no husband and evidently her family had disowned her because she had no resources at all. Jesus painted this woman on the canvass of God's Word for all time. Jesus enshrined this poor widow woman in the Word of God for eternity; not with a name, but with just the identification of what she gave. She put in two mites, approximately a penny.

*Jesus enshrined this poor widow woman in the Word of God for eternity; not with a name, but with just the identification of what she gave.*

Jesus called His disciples over to see this. He had a lesson for them. He said that she had cast in more than any of those who had gone before her. I can see Peter scratching his head because this made no sense at all. The lady had only put in two mites. Jesus explained that she gave more because all the others gave out of their abundance, but she gave out of her living. While the others gave out of their abundance, she gave out of her lunch money. She gave out of her living expenses.

## God Knows All

The text suggests that we are so concerned about what other people know, that we forget that God knows all. We are legitimately concerned about the loss of privacy in our society.

> *We are so concerned about what other people know, that we forget that God knows all.*

Anytime we use our credit cards, the information is entered into a database. The database has a record of where we ate and the hotel where we stayed. They might not know what we were doing, but they have a record anytime we use our credit cards. If God would put that kind of database into the mind of man and give him the ability to create it, what kind of database do you think He has?

Let me tell you how I feel about what others give. I care that they give, but I really don't care to know what they give. As pastor, sometimes it is necessary for me to know because of appointments to leadership positions, but I don't really care to know because one of the most difficult things in my ministry is having to fight back the agony of seeing on paper that the brother or sister who comes every Sunday praising God and jumping up and down singing I Love You, Lord is giving nothing. I don't need that kind of agony. I have to fight back the pain of how much it hurts to see them strutting like those who strutted when Jesus was watching the treasury.

I am told that there were 13 treasuries that were made like trumpet horns. Those who gave "struttingly" would "zing" (toss) the coins in so they would make a lot of noise. Certain people of that day were known as "zingers." Jesus watched the zingers on that day. I don't care to know what others give, but God knows, and it is His gaze that counts.

## An Equal Opportunity God

Notice, God gave all of them an equal opportunity to give. He gives us an equal opportunity to serve and worship Him. He gives us an equal opportunity to demonstrate our love for Him. God gives us an equal opportunity to come into a perfect relationship with Him so we can be in the flow of His blessings regardless of our race, culture or economic status. We serve an equal opportunity God.

The tithe guarantees an equal sacrifice rather than equal gifts.

> *The tithe guarantees an equal sacrifice rather than equal gifts. If God required equal gifts, He would not be an equal opportunity God.*

If God required equal gifts, He would not be an equal opportunity God. If I make $50,000 and and you make $20,000 and you're required to give the same gift that I give, that would not be fair. If you make $100,000 and I only make $35,000 and I'm required to give the same gift that you make, that would not be fair. God has leveled the playing field. He says give a tenth. A tenth of $50,000 is $5,000 a year. A tenth of $20,000 is $2,000 a year. A tenth of $100,000 is $10,000 a year. A tenth of $35,000 is $3,500 a year. It's simple mathematics and it's fair. God is an equal opportunity God.

I find it interesting that those who disagree with me are usually on the upper end of the income scale. They say it's unfair because they have to give too much. They say, "I was a tither when I was making $10,000 a year. I tithed when I was making $20,000 a year. When I moved up to $50,000, I got a little slack, but I was close. When I moved up to $100,000 a year, I stopped tithing because it was just too much to give." Let me tell you what God is saying to you, "If you are having problems tithing at $50,000, $75,000 or $100,000, I will be happy to take you back to $10,000 where you can feel a bit more comfortable." God is an equal opportunity God.

## Giving is a Necessary Part of Worship

There are several spiritual truths in Jesus' lesson. One of the first things we learn from this message is that giving is a necessary part of worship. It is inconceivable to *Giving is a necessary part of worship.* think about worshipping God without giving. The voice of the prophet spoke to us at the church where I pastor about ten years ago when we were budgeting for our revival. Since we budget for revival, we don't take up a collection during revival. Some of us were proud that we didn't take up a collection, until we realized we can't worship without giving.

The very first act of worship was not a sermon or a song. Cain and Abel, out of the very instinct that God had put in them, built an altar and gave. This is nothing new that we do. It is not a novelty that we have a treasury. God's house, and God's people have always had a treasury and given an offering. We cannot worship without giving. It is a necessary part of worship.

## Money is Condensed Life

Money is condensed life. It sounds almost sinful to say that, but Jesus knew it. That is why He spent so much time talking about it in the Bible. He talked about money all the time. We skirt over money because we don't want to hear it, but that is why Jesus spent His last forty-eight hours sitting and watching what people gave.

Money is condensed life. Just like condensed milk or con-

_____
*Money is condensed life.*         centrated juice, it is pent up energy. It
_____
is what this poor widow woman had as her only identification. We don't know her name. The only thing we know about her is what she gave. Suppose what we gave was written in the Book of Life by our names. How would it read? Be assured that God's database has the record because God watches what we give to the church.

Actually, our giving is the best index of our commitment. The moment of truth is every time the offering tray is passed. Every time the offering tray is passed, God watches and judgment takes place. All I'm saying is that if we believe in the risen Lord and the Word of God, then we should know and feel His gaze upon our hearts every time the offering is passed.

## Less is Not Least and Most is Not Best

A third spiritual truth is: Less is not necessarily the least and the most is not necessarily the best. That ought to encourage some of us and make others mad. Jesus does not deal in net amounts. He weighs what we give in relation to our blessings. He weighs what you give in relation to the amount from which it was taken. How big is your blessing pile? How good is your job? What kind of house do you live in? What kind of car do you drive? How much is in your bank account? How much do you bring home compared to others? Jesus weighs what we give in relation to our pile. If we consider what we give in relation to our pile, we can then determine if Jesus is gazing with a smile or a frown.

*Less is not necessarily the least and the most is not necessarily the best.*

The Bible tells us that Jesus can be grieved; the Holy Spirit grieves (Eph. 4:30a). If I have to fight back the pain, when I see people not giving, how much pain and grief do you think Jesus has to fight back? God watches what we give. What counts in God's ledger is the sacrifice. Are you giving sacrificially? God knows.

## Summary

God watches what we give to the church. Give so that you can worship him properly. Give to please God. Do not worry about what others may think about what you give. God knows your ability. He knows what you have because He gave it to you. Give sacrificially out of your living and out of your love for the Lord, and God will bless you.

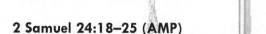

**2 Samuel 24:18–25 (AMP)**

¹⁸Then God came to David and said, Go up, rear an altar to the LORD on the threshing floor of Araunah the Jebusite. ¹⁹So David went up according to Gad's word, as the LORD commanded. ²⁰Araunah looked and saw the king and his servants coming toward him; and [he] went out and bowed himself before the king with his face to the ground. ²¹Araunah said, Why has my lord the king come to his servant? And David said, To buy the threshing floor from you, to build there an altar to the LORD, that the plague may be stayed from the people. ²²And Araunah said to David, Let my lord the king take and offer up what seems good to him. Behold, here are oxen for burnt sacrifice, and threshing instruments and the yokes of the oxen for wood. ²³All this, O king, Araunah gives to the king. And Araunah said to the king, The LORD your God accept you. ²⁴But King David said to Araunah, No, but I will buy it of you for a price. I will not offer burnt offerings to the LORD my God of that which costs me nothing. So David bought the threshing floor and the oxen for fifty shekels of silver. ²⁵David built there an altar to the LORD and offered burnt offerings and peace offerings. So the LORD heeded the prayers for the land, and Israel's plague was stayed.

# I Will Not Serve the Lord With That Which Costs Me Nothing:
## Living on Welfare in the Church

It has come to my attention that many church folks are living on welfare in the church. Also, many church folks are attempting to serve God with that which costs them nothing. If you think I'm not talking to you, know that God is talking to each of us. He is specifically talking to two categories of Christians—those who give what they think they can afford and those who think they cannot afford to give anything.

Our outlook determines our outcome. If our outlook, that is our motive, is giving only to support the programs of the church, we will give what we can afford and those who cannot afford anything will give nothing. If we are honest, most of us give what we can afford and those who cannot afford to give any-

> Many church folks are living on welfare in the church.

thing, give nothing. However, if our outlook is that we are giving to worship God, then those who give what they can afford will give more and everybody will give something.

## An Invitation to Worship

In our text from 2 Samuel 24, David was invited by God to worship Him. Verse 18 says, *"Go up, rear an altar to the LORD on the threshing floor of Araunah the Jebusite."* In other words, God invited David to worship Him at a specific place—on the threshing floor of Araunah, the Jebusite—and at a specific time. Perhaps, we will better understand the spiritual truths if we examine the entire text beginning at the tenth verse.

David's conscience began to bother him after he took a census. He asked the Lord, "What did I do wrong?" King David,

*Making comparisons with others steals God's glory.*

who knew the Lord, had counted the people. I don't know what the problem was, but I believe that we need to be careful with how we use numbers. How many members are in the church? How many members are enrolled in Fulfillment Hour (Sunday School)? How big is your budget? Making comparisons with others steals God's glory. Numbers can be very dangerous, particularly in the church, when we use them to boast about ourselves and compare ourselves with others who may have lesser numbers. Maybe David had counted all of the people in his army because he wanted to have the biggest army. Maybe he wanted to brag about how many people were in all of Israel and Judea to show that he had the biggest kingdom. Whatever the reason, his conscience bothered him and he had to go to the Lord and ask what he had done wrong.

The Lord sent His prophet, Gad. In those days, all of the kings had a prophet as their contact man. Gad told David that he had done wrong and that God was giving him three choices: "I will send a famine on the land, I will have your enemies run you down for about three months or I will send a plague on the land" (2 Sam.24:13). David knew this was a hard thing, and he knew that he didn't want men on his trail. So David replied: "I'll take your punishment, Lord. Whatever you do, I don't want man's justice. I will take your grace" (2 Sam. 24:14). David knew that man's justice would strike him down, but God's grace would lift him up. So David decided to take the plague rather than have his enemies on his tail.

A plague came upon the land and wiped out people. David sought the Lord asking why so many people were dying when "It is I who sinned against you" (2 Sam. 24:17). The Lord stopped the plague just before it reached the holy city of Jerusalem. Before He stopped it, He invited David to worship. He invited David to go down to the threshing floor of Araunah the Jebusite and worship Him in the middle of the plague, not afterward (2 Sam. 24:18).

David went to the threshing floor of Araunah. When Araunah saw the king, he ran out and asked why was he there. David said that he wanted to build an altar for God. Araunah said, "No problem. I will give you the wood. I will give you the oxen. I will help you build the fire. I will start the fire for you. I will give you instruments for the fire. Whatever you need, I will give you" (2 Sam. 24:22–23). David said, "No way! I don't want you to give it to me. I will buy it. I can't worship the Lord with that which costs me nothing" (2 Sam. 24:24). David was saying he did not want to be a welfare recipient in the church. He did not want to serve God with that which cost him nothing. David refused to have free worship. David said, "I refuse to worship the Lord with that which costs me nothing." The authorized version of the text says "For I will not serve the Lord with that which costs me nothing" (2 Sam. 24:24). The origin of the root word serve is "worship." David was saying, "I cannot worship the Lord with that which costs me nothing." Giving God that which costs us something is an outgrowth of a desire to worship God as He intended to be worshiped.

## Welfare Worship

Our problem lies in what I call "welfare worship." Welfare worship is when you try to worship God with that which costs you nothing. Most people choose their church based on their personal needs. Most of us, when we look for a church home, choose one that will satisfy us rather than looking for a church that is fulfilling the purposes of God. We come to a church to try

> *Welfare worship is when you try to worship God with that which costs you nothing.*

it out, to see if we are comfortable and if it meets our needs. Instead, we need to look for a church that fulfills the five-fold purpose of God—evangelism, discipleship, ministry/missions, fellowship and worship.

I know we feel that the church has to be right for us. No, it doesn't! It's not about us! It's all about God! It is about underwriting the ministries of the church. It is not about numbers or being the biggest and the best. It is not about satisfying our personal needs. It is about worshiping God who:

1. Created us to worship Him.

2. Invites us to worship.

3. Enjoys our worshiping Him.

4. Is worthy of our worship.

5. When we understand that it's about God and not about us, we will get off of welfare.

## Premier Welfare Recipients

Among those who are living on welfare in the church, is a group I call the "premier welfare recipients." They go around looking for a free church. They remind me of the person who is always driving around looking for a parking meter that has not expired. They want to park on someone else's dime. They don't want to use the talents that God gave them. They don't want to give any money. During the praise and worship service, they look like they are trying to preserve energy. The energy we have comes from God. The breath we have comes from God. It all belongs to God. It takes energy to praise God. We have to worship Him in spirit and in truth (John 4:24). Some of us have all energy and no money. Some of us have a little money and a little energy. Some of us have no energy and no money. When we worship Him in spirit and in truth, we must worship Him with our energy and our financial resources.

## A Bothersome Conscience

If we love the Lord and show our love to Him through worship, our consciences will bother us when we sin (not if we sin, but when we sin). If we love the Lord and show our love to Him with some energy in worship and truth in giving, then our consciences will bother us when we sin. Second Samuel 24:10 says that it was after David took the census that his conscience began to bother him. David knew the Lord. The Lord brought him from the sinful world of adultery with Bathsheba and the murder of Uriah. When he sinned, his conscience bothered him.

*If we love the Lord and show our love to Him through worship, our consciences will bother us when we sin.*

We cannot come to church on Sunday, feed on God's Word, praise Him, worship Him in spirit and in truth, and then go sleep around without our consciences bothering us. We cannot gossip and allow our anger to be out of control without it bothering us. We can't even hide our praise without our consciences bothering us. (It has come to me that maybe some folks don't worship Him because they don't want to be bothered.)

## Worship in the Midst of Trouble

God wants us to worship Him even in the midst of trouble. It was not when the plague was over, but in the midst of the plague that God invited David to worship Him on the threshing floor.

*God wants us to worship Him even in the midst of trouble.* Many of us think we should worship Him only when we have been delivered. God wants us to worship Him while we are in the delivery room. Some of us are going through trials and tribulations right now and we need to know that we are in the delivery room. Some of us are catching hell on our jobs or in our homes. We need to understand that we are in the delivery room and if we muster up a little energy and a little money to worship God in spirit and in truth, God will deliver us in the midst of our trouble.

## God Invites Worship Even When He is Not Pleased

**God invites us to worship Him even when He is not pleased with our behavior**. He invited David to worship Him even though David had done wrong in numbering the people and stealing God's glory. Although David had sinned, God said, "I want you to worship me right now on the threshing floor of Araunah." Some of us know we have done  *God answers prayer in the* something wrong in God's eyes. Like David,  *midst of worship.* we sinned before God and man. We know what we have done. We know our thoughts. Yet, in the midst of all that, God is saying, "Worship Me." He created us to worship Him. He enjoys our worshiping Him and He is worthy of our worship.

God answers prayer in the midst of worship. In verse 25, David built an altar and gave a burnt offering and a peace offering to the Lord. God answered his prayer and the plague stopped. God answers prayer in the midst of worship. If you have been praying for a breakthrough or deliverance, I want you to know that God answers prayer in the midst of worship. We need to worship Him.

God invites us to worship Him regardless of the time or place. Second Samuel 24:16 says that the angel of Lord was on the threshing floor of Araunah, the Jebusite, with his hand stretched to destroy Jerusalem when God answered David's prayer and stopped the plague. Well this is our threshing floor and this is our time. God is inviting us to worship Him right now for this is the time and the place.

## Summary

We cannot worship God with that which costs us nothing. Our giving expresses our love for God. We can no longer afford to live on welfare in the church. We should not want a free church or even a cheap preacher. Our desire should be to worship God, our creator with the best we have to give. No more can we give what we think we can afford. No more can we give nothing. When we sincerely desire to worship God, we will want to give the Lord that which costs us something.

**Luke 19:12–27(NKJV)**

12Therefore He said: "A certain nobleman went into a far country to receive for himself a kingdom and to return. 13So he called ten of his servants, delivered to them ten minas, and said to them, "Do business till I come.' 14But his citizens hated him, and sent a delegation after him, saying, "We will not have this man to reign over us.'

15"And so it was that when he returned, having received the kingdom, he then commanded these servants, to whom he had given the money, to be called to him, that he might know how much every man had gained by trading. 16Then came the first, saying, "Master, your mina has earned ten minas.' 17And he said to him, "Well done, good servant; because you were faithful in a very little, have authority over ten cities.' 18And the second came, saying, "Master, your mina has earned five minas.' 19Likewise he said to him, "You also be over five cities.'

20Then another came, saying, "Master, here is your mina, which I have kept put away in a handkerchief. 21For I feared you, because you are an austere man. You collect what you did not deposit, and reap what you did not sow."

*continued on page 86*

**Luke 19:12–27 (NKJV)continued**

²²And he said to him, "Out of your own mouth I will judge you, you wicked servant. You knew that I was an austere man, collecting what I did not deposit and reaping what I did not sow. ²³Why then did you not put my money in the bank, that at my coming I might have collected it with interest?"

²⁴And he said to those who stood by, "Take the mina from him, and give it to him who has ten minas." ²⁵(But they said to him, "Master, he has ten minas.") ²⁶"For I say to you, that to everyone who has will be given; and from him who does not have, even what he has will be taken away from him. ²⁷But bring here those enemies of mine, who did not want me to reign over them, and slay them before me."

# Are You a Good Steward?

Stewardship time is a time of self-examination and self-evaluation. We are to examine ourselves in the mirror of God's Word. We examine ourselves in the mirror at home to see how we look. That is exactly what God is calling us to do with His Word. His Word is a mirror to us. God wants us to examine ourselves in the light of the question, Are you a good steward?

The question is personal. Not is your neighbor a good steward, but are *you* a good steward? When we hear the Word of God, we have a tendency to look outward rather than inward. I experience it all the time when husbands and wives come to different services. One may come to the 8 o'clock service and the other to the 11 o'clock service. After the

*Stewardship time is a time of self-examination and self-evaluation.*

8 o'clock service, one might come up to me and say, "What a good sermon! I sure hope my husband or wife comes to the 11 o'clock service because he or she needs to hear this." This message is one of self-examination. It is for you to look inward.

## What is a Steward?

A steward is someone who manages or takes care of something that does not belong to him. Like a babysitter takes care of a baby that does not belong to them. When we leave our baby with the babysitter it is very obvious and everybody knows that the baby does not belong to the babysitter. The baby belongs to the parent. When the parent comes back he expects to find

*A steward is someone who manages or takes care of something that does not belong to him.*

the baby in good shape. He expects the baby to be fed, dry, not abused or misused. Well, God has left us to do some church sitting and He is coming back again for His church, for His bride. He expects His bride to be unblemished, well fed and not messed up, abused or misused. He has left us to be stewards over His church.

Every Christian is a steward. There is no such thing as a non-steward Christian. We are either bad stewards or good stewards.

There is no middle ground. In the parable of the talent in Matthew 25, it talks about an unprofitable steward or a profitable steward. We are one or the other. There is no in-between. All of us want to please Him. So the question is, Are you a good steward or a bad steward? If you are not pleasing God, then you are a bad steward.

## Personal Spiritual Development

The ultimate goal of personal stewardship is personal spiritual development. In other words, we are not talking about money. We are talking about spiritual development, building Christian character, growing up in His likeness, and being most like Him. We are talking about being better Christians and pleasing him.

> *The ultimate goal of personal stewardship is personal spiritual development.*

All of us want to please Him. In 1 Corinthians, we are told that a good steward is found faithful. It is impossible to please God without faith.

In the book of Hebrews, there is a roll call of faith. It says that by faith Enoch was taken away so he did not see death. Before he was taken, he had this testimony: *"He pleased God...without faith, it is impossible to please Him"* (Heb.11:5-6).

Those who are among that great cloud of witnesses that are looking down (be it your mother or father, Enoch or Abraham) had the testimony of pleasing God before leaving this earth. They would not be among the witnesses if they had not had this testimony. For it is impossible to please God without faith.

I must remind you that spiritual development begins with repentance. We will never grow unless we first repent. We need to make a decision to do better and in order to do that we must first repent. We can't just say, "I'll do better." We must repent by acknowledging that God is right and we are wrong, and then apologize to Him for our disobedience and commit to do better.

## Terrorists in the Church

There are only three characters in the parable in Luke 19—the nobleman who represents God, the good steward and the enemy. Notice, God says if we are not good stewards, then we are enemies, terrorists. Yes, there are terrorists in the church. If we are not good stewards, we are one of the "Bins":

- **"Bin Hiding"** has been hiding from the preacher and the Fulfillment Hour Shepherd (Sunday School Teacher). He has been hiding his praise and his stewardship.

- **"Bin Napping"** has been napping during praise time, offering and through all the stewardship sermons. He even naps during the invitation.

- **"Bin Complaining"** has been complaining about everything. He's been complaining about the stewardship messages. He's been complaining that the church is growing too fast. He's been complaining about the music. He's been complaining about a little of everything.

- Then there are the twins, **"Bin Doing Nothing"** and **"Bin Giving Nothing."** Bin Doing Nothing is the number one terrorist in the church. He has been doing absolutely nothing, nowhere in the church. "Bin Giving Nothing" has been giving no time, no talent, no gifts and no money—nothing to the unified budget and nothing to the capital campaign.

> Bin Doing Nothing is the number one terrorist in the church.

Are you a good steward or a terrorist? I'm so glad that there are some other "Bins" in the church. There are some righteous, holy Bins: "Bin Working" and "Bin Serving" have been working to show themselves approved. There are others, too—Bin Giving, Bin Singing, Bin Praising, Bin Tithing and Bin Blessed. I want to be Bin Blessed. Don't you?

## It's the Lord's House

Stewards are servants in the Master's house, not guests. We are laborers, not landlords. Stewards are for churches. Churches are not for stewards. Some of us think that the church is here to satisfy our needs, but we are here to satisfy the needs of the church. We don't own the church. It's the Lord's church. It doesn't make any difference if our granddaddy was the founder,

*Stewards are for churches. Churches are not for stewards.*

or our great-granddaddy was chairman of the deacons for fifty years or our father pastored the church for the last forty-five years. It's the Lord's church.

## Are You a Good Steward?

Are you a good steward? Are you serving the church's purposes? Let's see. Examine yourself against these principles:

1. **A good steward takes ownership of the church's vision and purposes.** A steward does not own the church, but a steward can own the vision. God gives the visions. As good stewards, we are to take ownership of that vision and work to bring it to fruition.

2. **A good steward disperses the goods of the church according to the purposes of God.** Again, the steward does not lean to his own understanding in the dispensation of any of the Master's resources. He manages everything according to God's purposes. He disperses the goods of the church, not according to his desires, but according to the purposes of God.

3. **A good steward is the guardian of the Master's family.** The church is the Master's family and our family of faith. So a good steward will not let anybody talk about the Master's family. A good steward will not let anybody talk about an unwed mother in the Master's family and won't participate in the conversation. A good steward won't let anybody talk about the preacher or the preacher's wife. A good steward will not permit or participate in anything that hurts God's family.

4. **A good steward is a steward of the mysteries of God (1 Cor. 4:1).** What are the mysteries of God? The first mystery is the gospel. It is how God would love His people so much that He would take on Sonship, robe

Himself in flesh, step down out of eternity, minister and heal for thirty-three years, go to a cross, die a criminal's death, and be raised again on the third day—these are mysteries. It's the foolishness of the cross that men are yet saved by their belief (1 Cor. 1:18). As good stewards, we are to be stewards of God's mysteries.

5. **A good steward is required to be faithful.** A good steward is required, not expected, to be faithful (1 Cor. 4:2). God does not judge those who go out witnessing by whether or not anybody gets saved. God looks at the fact that they went. He judges them on their faithfulness, not on their success.

Likewise, God doesn't judge my preaching on whether or not anybody ever gets saved, joins the church or tithes. God judges me on whether I'm faithful in rightly delivering His word. I struggled with that when I first became pastor twenty-three years ago. It bothered me that people would shake my hand, say they liked the sermon, and then go back to living the same way they were living. God spoke to me on this and told me that He was judging me on my faithfulness to preach His word.

**6. A good steward pays God first.** God wants us to be good stewards of our money. He tells us a story in Luke 19 about investments, banking, trading and money, but that is not what the story is about. Why would God tell us a story about money, banking and trading? About how much money we can make and how we do good business? He knows that we identify with money. He knows that some of us love money. *"For the love of money is the root of all evil" (1 Tim. 6:10).* He tells us in His Word, *"where your treasure is, there will your heart be also" (Matt. 6:21).* A good steward pays Him first. It's the principle of the first-fruit. Your checkbook will tell you whom you love.

## The Parable of the Ten Pounds

In Luke 19, we find a story about a nobleman. The nobleman is God. The nobleman went into a far country to claim his kingdom and then came back. There were some citizens of the country who went after him and hated him and said, "We don't want this man to reign over us." Then the parable says that God gave one mina to each of ten servants and told them to do business.

(The New King James uses the word minas. The authorized King James uses pounds.)

He left as a nobleman, got his kingdom and came back as a king. When He returned, He asked his servants for a report. "How were your investments? What kind of trading did you do?" One said, "I took that one pound and now I have ten pounds." God said, "Thou good and faithful servant. For that one pound I will give you ten cities." Another servant said, "I have five pounds." God said, "I will give you five cities." There was one servant, like too many of us, who took his one pound and didn't even put it in the bank. In the bank, he would have gotten a little interest. He didn't put it in a passbook savings account, a CD or mutual funds. He said, "I hid it." The Lord said, "I will judge you out of your own mouth. Out of your own mouth are you condemned" (Luke 19:22). He also said, "By the way, go get those who hated me, my enemies. They will be slain." When God comes again, He will put His enemies to death.

## Why Are We Bad Stewards?

Why are some of us bad stewards? Some of us are bad stewards because we are lazy and some of us are bad stewards because we are rejecting God. Laziness is a spirit from which many of us need to be delivered. In Proverbs 6, we are told to be like the ant. It is not a sluggard. The ant works day and night, but we are lazy.

How are we lazy? We're being lazy when we don't determine what we are going to give God before getting to church. Instead we lazily wait for the offering tray to be passed around and then we think about giving. We're lazy when we won't take the time to accurately calculate 10 percent of our income. We're just too lazy to do the math. Finally, we're lazy with our time and energy. We would rather watch TV than

*Some of us are bad stewards because we are lazy and some of us are bad stewards because we are rejecting God.*

work in the kingdom. The scriptures tell us to work while the day is young because the night will come when no man can work (John 9:4). In Matthew 25:26a, God says, "You wicked and lazy servant. You are just lazy."

In Luke 19:14, his citizens hated him, and sent a delegation after him, saying, *"We will not have this man to reign over us."* God wants to be Lord of our lives. Don't reject Him. Give the Lord your life. If He has you, He will have yours.

## Godly Instruction

God instructs us on how to be good stewards. That is what the parable of the ten pounds is about. God is teaching us, not about making money, but about spiritual character. He is teaching us about the whole matter of our money, gifts, talents, time and faithfulness. The matter of trading is about what we do with them. Do we invest them in the Lord? The Lord God is coming again and we will be held accountable. We have no excuse because God has given us instructions.

*God instructs us on how to be good stewards.*

## A Good Steward is Tested

A good steward is tested. He is first tested with a small amount. The servants in the parable were given only a pound. Today that would be equivalent to about a dollar. He said, "If you are faithful over these few dollars, I will give you a lot more." We need to understand that God will test every Christian's work. First Corinthians 3 tells us that every man's work will be tested by fire. It is a misunderstanding to think that only sinners will be judged. God's servants will be judged according to the work we have done and how we used our gifts. He will judge us on whether or not we treated them as if they were gold, silver and precious stones.

## A Good Steward is Blessed

A good steward is blessed. It not only pays to serve God, but it pays well. For each dollar the good stewards gave God, He gave them a city. How can a dollar buy a city? In Alabama, we used to call that "good money." A dollar for a city! It not only pays to serve God. It pays awfully well!

## Summary

If we are faithful over the mysteries of God, and over the mystery of His return, God will bless us. Look at what the text says:

> *"Blessed are those servants whom the master, when he comes, will find watching [faithful, working, serving]. Assuredly, [not doubtfully] I say to you that he will gird himself and have them sit down to eat, and will come and serve them" (Luke 12:37 NKJV).*

God Himself will serve His good servants. If I am found faith-ful, a holy God is going to serve a wretch like me. He is just that good. He is faithful to keep every one of His promises. He promises that He will come, sit them down and serve those who are found faithful. I want to be a good steward. I want to sit down at the table and hear His voice say, *"Well done, thou good and faithful servant; thou hast been faithful over a few things"* *(Matt. 25:21)*.

**Matthew 6:24-32 (NIV)**

$^{24}$No one can serve two masters. Either he will hate the one and love the other, or he will be devoted to the one and despise the other. You cannot serve both God and Money. $^{25}$Therefore I tell you, do not worry about your life, what you will eat or drink; or about your body, what you will wear. Is not life more important than food, and the body more than clothes? $^{26}$Look at the birds of the air; they do not sow or reap or store away in barns, and yet your heavenly Father feeds them. Are you not much more valuable than they? $^{27}$Who of you by worrying can add a single hour to his life? $^{28}$And why do you worry about clothes? See how the lilies of the field grow. They do not labor or spin. $^{29}$Yet I tell you that not even Solomon in all his splendor was dressed like one of these. $^{30}$If that is how God clothes the grass of the field, which is here today and tomorrow is thrown into the fire, will he not much more clothe you, O you of little faith? $^{31}$So do not worry, saying, "What shall we eat?" or "What shall we drink?" or "What shall we wear?" $^{32}$For the pagans run after all these things, and your heavenly Father knows that you need them.

**Matthew 6:33**

But seek ye first the kingdom of God, and his righteousness; and all these things shall be added unto you.

# Put God First in Your Life:

## Keep on Matthew 6:33ing

In our culture, we are obsessed with the question: Who's number one? When the University of Michigan football team plays against Ohio State University, and when Florida State University plays against the University of Florida, the question is asked, Who's number one? Will Michigan be number one or will it be Ohio State? Will Florida State be number one or will it be Florida? Not only do we want to know "Who's number one?" in football, but also in entertainment. Who's number one on the rhythm and blues chart? Who's number one in country and western music? We always want to know who and what is number one. Who's the number one richest man in the world? What's the number one car? I would like to raise another question: Who is number one in our lives? I challenge us to put God first in our lives and to keep on "Matthew 6:33ing." That is, keep seeking God's kingdom first and all other things will be added unto us.

## Firstfruit Giving

If we put God first in our lives, He will provide all we need. However, we must first understand what the Bible has to say about firstfruit giving, the principle of giving to God first. In Deuteronomy 26:1–2, Moses explained the festival of the first-fruit to the people. He reminded them to take the firstfruit of everything when they went into the promised land. They were

*If we put God first in our lives, He will provide all we need.*

instructed to put the firstfruits of the soil in a basket and take them to the place God had chosen. We don't ritually celebrate a feast of the first-fruit because of all that we are in Christ. Yet, there should be a time when we look at where the Lord has brought us from.

The firstfruits are part of worship. I believe He deserves the firstfruits. I believe we need to put God first in our lives. We need to bring Him the best of all that we have including the strength of our youth. I'm old enough to understand what the strength of our youth really is. Now that my hair is gray, I'm old enough to know that I'm not as strong as I was during my youth. I can't do the things I could do when I was twenty-five, but I can remember the strength of my youth. I could walk faster, run faster, jump higher and fight more when I was twenty-five. We want to give God our very best. That's our first-fruit.

## Out of Order

The problem is that we have what I call an "out of order syndrome." We have things first that should be last and things last that should be first. We have the cart before the horse. We have the wagon in front of the mule and the tail wagging the dog, rather than the dog wagging the tail. We have things out of order, which means our lives are out of order. It seems as though some of us should have an "OUT OF ORDER - DO NOT USE" sign hung around our necks. "Out of order" can be interpreted as out of fellowship with God. "Out of order" can also be interpreted as out of a perfect relationship with God or out of the will of God. Let's see what the scripture teaches us so we can get in order.

*The problem is that we have what I call an "out of order syndrome."*

## Sweating the Small Things

The first thing the scripture teaches us is that when we put God first in our lives, we don't have to sweat the small stuff because we realize that it's all small stuff. Somebody sweats about what outfit to wear to Church. Somebody is sweating now about what's going to happen on the job tomorrow. Somebody is sweating about his or her disobedient children. When we truly put God first, we don't have to sweat the small stuff because we realize everything is small stuff compared to God. What we wear or eat is small stuff. How we may live or what house we live in is small stuff. If we put God first, we won't have so much turmoil and anxiety in our lives and we shouldn't because we are saved.

*We don't have to sweat the small stuff because we realize that it's all small stuff.*

This is not a question of salvation. We know if we are saved, but evidently we don't know how to put our Savior first. When we put God totally first, when we keep Matthew 6:33ing Him, we will continually seek Him and His righteousness, and we won't have so much anxiety or all that worry. The New Testament scripture tells us to look at the birds and the lilies. They are not worried about their food. They are not worried about who is going to clothe them. Doesn't God value us more than He does a bird, a piece of grass or a lily in the field? After all, the Bible tells us that the man and woman is God's crowning glory. If you believe that, then seek first the kingdom of God and all these other things—food, clothing, shelter, etc.—will be added unto you.

## Where is Our Treasure?

The second thing the scripture teaches us is that where our treasure is, there we will find our hearts also. We shouldn't be surprised at the awesome knowledge of *God is telling us to look in our* God. He is omniscient, all knowing. God *checkbooks and we will see* knows that we love material things. God *whom we love.* knows that we love money, so He doesn't skirt around it. He talks to us about it in His Bible.

In modern terms, God is telling us to look in our checkbooks and we will see whom we love. Is the very first bill written to the local church? It should be. Before we pay the light bill, mortgage, car note, etc., our first check should be to God. It should also go to the place that He has designated as "mine house," which is the local church. That's what our checkbooks should look like. Who do we pay first? Are we "out of order"?

I heard some interesting comments and found that some of our young people paid their cellular phone and cable television bill before paying anything else. Before they paid the rent, they paid their cellular phone and cable television bills. Is that extremely "out of order"?

We must keep on Matthew 6:33ing Him. If we seek first the kingdom of God, all these other things will be added unto us. God said *all*, not some, but *all* of these other things would be added unto us. God gives us His best; therefore we should give Him our best.

## Leftovers

We need to give God our firstfruits, not our leftovers. God does not give us leftovers. Morning by morning, He gives us new mercies. Isn't that wonderful that He doesn't give us leftover

> We need to give God our firstfruits, not our leftovers.

mercies? He doesn't give us mercies from the Salvation Army or Goodwill. He doesn't even give us mercies leftover in the refrigerator. Morning by morning, God sends us new mercies from heaven.

Keep on Matthew 6:33ing. Seek first the kingdom of God and all these other things will be added unto us.

## Serving Two Masters

Scripture clearly tells us that we cannot serve two masters. If we try to serve two masters, we are going to serve one and despise the other. We cannot serve God and material things. There is no halfway. In 1973, I was serving material things. I would pull up to my house in Shaker Heights, Ohio in my 1973 Eldorado with a cavalier roof and just sit there. I had a piece of the American pie and was so happy about it, but it took a failed business and an addiction to alcohol to show me that I couldn't serve two masters. I am a witness that we cannot serve God and wealth. God gave us a promise and I'm a testimony that if we seek God's kingdom first, all other things will be added unto us.

## Summary

God is an equal opportunity God, and there is no reason why we, the body of Christ, should not commit to what He asks of us in relation to stewardship. There is no reason why we should not commit to stewardship except that there is rebellion within us.

Stewardship is about our relationship with God. It is about raising the faith of the Church individually and collectively. When we raise our faith, we grow spiritually.

If we put God first, trust and have faith in Him, God will take care of us. The whole matter of tithing is not a money matter. It's a faith matter. We are holding on to the tree trunk when God wants us to go out on the limb. He will take care of us when our barrel is bare and when it is full. He'll take care of us when we are down and out and when we prosper, when we are up and when we get knocked down. **Just keep on Matthew 6:33ing and God will take care of you.**

**Matthew 6:33**

But seek ye first the kingdom of God, and his righteousness; and all these things shall be added unto you.

# Jesus Christ, "Prime Time":

## Putting First Things First

I asked somebody, "What does it mean to you when you hear the words 'prime time'?" He told me he thought of a football player named Dion Sanders. I asked, "Why do you think of Dion?" He said, "Because he can run a 140 yards in 4.2 seconds." Well, I told him that Jesus can run it in zero flat, so certainly we ought to call Him "Prime Time."

Someone else told me that "prime time" means the choice spot on television for commercials because it's when the most people give their attention. I said that all the attention ought to be on Jesus, so certainly I can call Him "Prime Time." During the Super Bowl, which is TV's most prime time, it costs millions of dollars for just seconds of advertising time. Now, that's prime time! **We should be able to give Jesus that kind of prime time.**

## Putting First Things First

Christians ought to be about the business of putting first things first. Sometimes we get it backwards and put other things in front of what Christians ought to put first. We sing "...for the rest of my life I'm going to serve Him..." and "Jesus, you're the center of my joy..." but what we say is authenticated only by what we do.

## Put the Bible First

The first thing we should put first is the Bible. The Bible ought to be the first book we read. There are lots of books out there by great authors and poets, but the Bible is our instruction manual for Christian living. The Bible ought to be the very first in our reading, even above our schoolbooks. We don't want to hear that because many of us have been to school and have a little formal education.

*The first thing we should put first is the Bible.*

I'm all for formal education. I went to school and I sent my sons to school, but the Bible came before any geography, social studies or math lesson. It is a poor excuse for parents to say that their child can't come to Bible study because he has to work on a project for school or has to study. That's a poor excuse. Let him *"seek ye first the kingdom of God, and his righteousness; and all these things shall be added unto you" (Matt 6:33).* Seek God first, and your geometry lesson will be added unto you.

One of the problems of today is that our parents are not training up our children. So when we wonder why children are shooting other children, it's because they haven't been given anything to fall back on. *"Train up a child in the way he should go: and when he is old, he will not depart from it" (Prov. 22:6).* The Bible doesn't say that when he goes to college, he won't depart from it. God knows us. We departed from it when we went to college. The Bible doesn't say when he goes into military service, he won't depart from it. We know that when we went into the Army, we departed from it. The Bible says when he is "old," he will have something to fall back on. We are raising a generation that has nothing to fall back on. If Christians are going to put first things first, we have to put reading the Bible first.

Another reason the Bible should be first is so we can hear from God. Some of us pray so fervently and we wonder why we don't get an answer. Basically, when we pray, we talk to

God. But when we read the Bible, God talks to us. The Bible is our guide. We need to put the Bible first.

## Put the Church First

The next thing that Christians should put first is the church. I don't care how spiritual we think the Masonic lodge or the Elks are, the church should come first. Our fraternity brothers and

*The next thing that Christians should put first is the church.*

our sorority sisters should not come before our brothers and sisters in Christ. We are losing our perspective when it comes to institutions. Christians ought to be about the business of putting first things first. The church is the only visible body of Christ that the world can see. We have to be about the business of cleaning it from the pulpit to the pews. Christ is coming back for His church and He wants His church adorned as a bride is prepared for her groom. The church has to be the first institution in our lives.

## Pay God First

Thirdly, **we have to put God first as we handle our money**. Get a mental picture of all your creditors, i.e., your bills. They may include your mortgage, Rich's-Macy's, Sears, MasterCard,

American Express, Visa, etc. Can you visualize all your creditors lined up to be paid? Now be very honest and ask yourself, "Where is God in that line?" If we are honest with ourselves, some of us will confess that God is not even in the line. So what does God get? Whatever is left. We say that He is the Rose of Sharon and the fairest of ten thousand, yet He's not in the line. My message is, seek ye first the kingdom of God. I'm asking that we move God to the front of the line. Let the first check you write be for "Prime Time"; not Prime Cable, but Jesus Christ, "Prime Time."

*Let the first check you write be for "Prime Time"; not Prime Cable, but Jesus Christ, "Prime Time."*

Let me tell you the secret to financial success: Pay God first, yourself second, and then everybody else. Are you going to be working hard all your life because you don't realize that money can work harder than you can work? Pay yourself, but first give God His dime and thank Him for letting you keep 90 cents. Then, pay yourself a dime and live off the remaining 80 cents. If you do this, you will have financial success. You will also have spiritual blessings all of your life. Try it. Put God first in your line.

## Put Relationships First

Last, but in no ways least, let me talk about our relationships—that is, our companions. Christians ought to be about the business of fellowshipping with Christians. We need each other. We have to go into a mean old world. Jesus went into it and we see how it treated Him. Christians need to fellowship with Christians so we can encourage and strengthen each other to face this world.

> *Christians need to fellowship with Christians so we can encourage and strengthen each other to face this world.*

Also, Christians ought to be about the business of marrying Christians. If we are unevenly yoked, we set ourselves up for hard times. The best companion is Jesus Christ. No better companion can we have than Jesus. We have to have a personal relationship with Him first, and then we can have a strong marriage relationship.

## Summary

Christians need to be about the business of putting Jesus Christ first in their lives. Make Jesus your "Prime Time"—that is, read your Bible, prepare the church for His return, pay God first and care for each other. When you do these things, all other things will be added unto you.

**Malachi 3:10**

Bring ye all the tithes into the storehouse, that there may be meat in mine house, and prove me now herewith, saith the LORD of hosts, if I will not open you the windows of heaven, and pour you out a blessing, that *there shall* not *be room* enough *to receive it.*

# An Offer Too Good to Refuse

What would you do if your CEO called you into his office and said "I can take you places if you will just be faithful, loyal and obedient to me. I will take care of you"? Some of us would jump on it. We would be the best flunkie any CEO ever had. We want to move up in life. We want blessings. The CEO is sitting in the big chair saying that if you're faithful to me, I will take you with me.

> God has made us an offer that is too good to refuse.

When we read Malachi 3:10, we realize that God has made us an offer that is too good to refuse. God, who is the Chief Executive Officer of the whole universe, the owner of everything, is saying, *"Prove me."* That means "try me." This is a spiritual matter. God is saying, "Step across the line of doubt into faith. Put your faith and your trust in me, and see if I won't take care of you. See if you won't move up the ladder with me. See if prosperity won't come your way. Try me!"

## A Matter of Faith, Not Money

Tithing is not a matter of money. It's a matter of faith. Tithing is not a money issue. It is a spiritual issue. I believe more people are saved during Stewardship Emphasis time than any other time during the year because money is the last thing some of us are holding on to before God can really use us.

We love our money. Jesus knew this. He said, *"For where your treasure is, there will your heart be also" (Matt 6:21 and Luke 12:34)*. Jesus knew we were going to love our money. Let me show you how right He was. Let's say you've been married a long time, and you love your wife, you love your husband.

*Tithing is not a money issue. It is a spiritual issue.*

What would you say if your spouse took $3,000 out of the bank account without telling you? You *thought* you loved him. You *thought* you loved her. We *know* we love our money.

## An Offer of Deliverance

You can be saved and still need delivering. God is saying, "I have an offer that is too good to refuse. I want to deliver you from your materialism." Note here that there is a difference between being saved and being delivered. You only have to be saved one time, but you can be delivered more than once, and from more than one thing. You only have to be saved from sin one time. Jesus didn't tell Nicodemus you must be born again and again and again. He just said, "Nicodemus, you must be born again" (John 3:3b).

From how many things have you been delivered? I can count some of my deliverances. Everybody knows that I was delivered from alcohol. I've been delivered from racism and prejudice. I've been delivered from looking at women as sex objects. With some men, everything they see is "Hmm, hmm. The Lord is my shepherd, I see what I want." Been there, done that! You need delivering.

I have also been delivered from materialism. I once worshiped things. I wanted to be a millionaire by the time I reached a certain age. I'm thankful today that if I lost my house, I wouldn't have an ounce of anxiety. I can stand before God and tell you that if my cars were gone, I wouldn't have any anxiety. Clothes are just material stuff. I no longer have one ounce of love for material stuff. It's interesting that when you get like that, God

*We don't create anything.*

*God is the creator.*

starts blessing you with material stuff. I need to tell you that because somebody needs deliverance from materialism.

Somebody needs deliverance from stinginess. Some people hoard things—that's stinginess! The Hebrew word *todah* means that we are "looking for a blessing with our hands cupped," but the word *yadah* means "thank you for deliverance with our hands extended and uplifted." We need to change the positions of our hands from a cup to praise. When our cup runs over and we can't hold anymore, we need to open up and just say, "Thank you, Lord."

## Look at God

I was in the grocery store the other day. As I was walking around I just said, "Look at God." When I saw the apples I thought, "Can I make an apple?" Can anybody make an apple? I didn't say make an apple pie, apple butter or apple cobbler.

We don't create anything. God is the creator. We don't know how to make an apple. I bought ten apples and began thinking about this deal that God offers us that is just too good to refuse. As I put the apples in a bag, I thought to myself, God said that out of these ten apples, I can have one, two, three, four, five, six, seven, eight, nine. "God, do you mean all you want is one?" I went on and picked up some sweet potatoes. Anybody can make a sweet potato pie, but who can make a potato? Only God. God is the creator. So I bought some sweet potatoes and once again I thought, "God said I can have one, two, three, four, five, six, seven, eight, nine sweet potatoes. All God wants is one." I went through the grocery store and found the special kind of milk my wife uses to make the lemon pies that I love. Now we know that a cow makes milk, but who makes the grass that the cow eats to make the milk? I bought some milk and thought to myself, here's one, two, three, four, five, six, seven, eight, nine containers of milk. "God, do you mean all you want is one?" As I shopped for other produce, I found myself praising and thanking Him for being the wonderful, generous creator He is.

When I finished shopping and pulled out my money to pay, I was reminded that the Lord blessed us with the exchange of money. Out of a $100, I can have $10, $20, $30, $40, $50, $60, $70, $80, $90 and all God wants is $10. We can't make an apple, a sweet potato or even milk. God has provided everything for us! It all belongs to Him! I looked at my groceries and thought, God is saying that all of this is mine and all He wants is one tenth, just a little bit. "God, You're too good! You've been better to me than I've been to myself." Look at God!

**Summary**

When I think, I can thank. When I think about the goodness of God, my soul cries out, "Hallelujah!" God is a good God. He is creator and owner of everything. He faithfully provides for our every need and in return He only asks that we acknowledge Him with a tenth of what's already His. God has made us an offer that is too good to refuse. Try Him and see if He won't pour you out a blessing that you will not have room enough to receive.

**2 Corinthians 8:7–14**

7Therefore, as ye abound in every *thing, in* faith, and utterance, and knowledge, and *in* all diligence, and *in* your love to us, *see* that ye abound in this grace also. 8I speak not by commandment, but by occasion of the forwardness of others, and to prove the sincerity of your love. 9For ye know the grace of our LORD Jesus Christ, that, though he was rich, yet for your sakes he became poor, that ye through his poverty might be rich. 10And herein I give *my* advice: for this is expedient for you, who have begun before, not only to do, but also to be forward a year ago. 11Now therefore perform the doing of *it*; that as *there was* a readiness to will, so *there may be* a performance also out of that which ye have. 12For if there be first a willing mind, *it is* accepted according to that a man hath, *and* not according to that he hath not. 13For I *mean* not that other men be eased, and ye burdened: 14But by an equality, *that* now at this time your abundance may be a supply for their want, that their abundance also *may be a supply* for your want: that there may be equality.

# Growing in the Grace of Giving

God speaks to us through Paul and some churches in Macedonia, a province of northern Greece. There were three churches in Macedonia—Thessalonica, Philipi and Berea. All three suffered great poverty. Paul told the church at Corinth that their mission was to help these churches spread the gospel. Paul said, "You have strong faith. You have learned to trust in the Lord. Not only do you sing the song *I Will Trust in the Lord*, but you live it. Not only that, but your preach-ing is pretty good. You are strong in the

*We're incomplete until we abound also in the grace of giving.*

utterance of the word. Your knowledge has grown. You have also grown in love for your minister." Then Paul said, "Although you've done all that, see that you abound in the grace of giving also" (2 Cor.8:7). God is saying that we're incomplete until we abound also in the grace of giving.

This message is "a call to missions" because the world is in desperate need. We wonder what's wrong with the world, and why we can't solve some of our political problems and environmental issues. There is a simple answer. The world does not know Jesus. We live in a capitalistic, free enterprise, greedy society. We will always be in need unless people come to know Jesus. So like our Corinthian brothers and sisters, we are called to grow in the grace of giving.

## Know the Spirit of the Macedonians

Paul says in 2 Cor 8:1, *"Moreover, brethren, we do you to wit of the grace of God bestowed on the churches of Macedonia."* We need to know the spirit of giving of these three churches. One of the great mysteries is in verse 2 which talks about how they gave. It says:

*"How that in a great trial of affliction the abundance of their joy and their deep poverty abounded unto the riches of their liberality" (2 Cor. 8:2).*

Now that's a tremendous contrast—great trials of affliction and abundance of joy. We don't normally think of affliction going with joy. The verse continues with *"their deep poverty abounded in the riches of their liberal giving."* We don't normally put poverty and the abundance of generosity together. Here we have three churches that suffered affliction and were in poverty, but were joyful and generous.

God is telling us to let the grace that the churches in Macedonia exhibited trickle down to us. The testimony of the Macedonian churches is that in their trials and tribulations, they had joy. In the midst of their poverty, they gave generously. Let that grace trickle down to all churches and God will bestow on us the same blessings that the churches in Macedonia received.

> We don't normally put poverty and the abundance of generosity together.

## Show the Sincerity of Your Love

God assumes a Missouri posture and says, "If you love me, show me." In my pastoral counseling of married couples, one of the main problems that wives complain about is that we husbands don't know how to show our love. Some of us husbands are still hanging on to the old song *If You Don't Know Me By Now.* Our wives are saying to us, "If you love me, show me. You say you love me, but you don't tell me. You say you love me, but you don't bring me flowers." If women feel that strongly about demonstrative love, how must God feel? How must God feel when some of us are still giving $5 and $10 a week? That's the old way. When some of us look at our percentage of giving, we are giving 1 or 2 percent of our total income to God. The challenge is to demonstrate the sincerity of our love.

## Know the Example of Christ

Christ gave. Second Corinthians 8:9 says:

*"For ye know the grace of our LORD Jesus Christ, that, though he was rich, yet for your sakes he became poor, that ye through his poverty might be rich."*

The Bible tells us that Jesus had everything in heaven. The book of Revelation says that all the heavenly beings worshiped Him. He had all heaven and all glory, but for our sake He became poor. God became incarnate in Jesus Christ. He left His glory in heaven to become man. Think about it. We're trying to get to heaven, and He left heaven.

*"For God so loved the world, that he gave his only begotten Son, that whosoever believeth in him should not perish, but have everlasting life" (John 3:16).*

God became a holy, humble man. The Lord took on flesh and blood and became a person of lowliness. The sovereign Lord became the subject. The beloved became the rejected. The perfect one became a sacrifice for sin. Life itself became a substitute for death. God gave. He didn't have to do it, but He did. Our challenge is to be like Him, to take on the mind of Christ that we might give also.

## Remember Your Past Record

*"And herein I give my advice: for this is expedient for you, who have begun before, not only to do, but also to be forward a year ago" (2 Cor. 8:10).* We can look at this from a positive or negative viewpoint. It was written from a positive viewpoint. This verse speaks about how we used to give. Many Christians today, who were once on fire for the Lord and understood the church to be the body of Christ, actually gave more then than they give now. That is what the true context of the scripture says. It says to think about when you started, and then complete what you started.

> Our challenge is to be like Him, to take on the mind of Christ that we might give also.

Many of us when asked to fill out commitment cards are saying, "I tried last year and I didn't make my commitment. I tried the year before and I didn't make my commitment." Try again! God blesses every one of your efforts. *"He who has begun a good work in you will complete it" (Phil. 1:6),* even if it has to be in heaven. Some of us have dropped off in our giving. You may think somebody is going to pick up the slack, but nobody can pick up the slack for you because God judges you.

> God blesses every one of your efforts.

We can also look at 2 Corinthians 8:10 from a negative viewpoint. Some of us know that we used to give God nothing or we might have given Him whatever we had in our pockets that was leftover after we had done everything else we wanted to do. Examine your record. Are you giving God leftovers?

### Give Readily and Willingly

God loves a cheerful giver. In verse 12 the scripture says, *"For if there be first a willing mind…"* **If you give grudgingly you might as well keep your money in your pocket.** The first criterion for acceptance is that you do it willingly. The second part of the verse 12 says, *"accepted according to that a man hath,* *and not according to that he hath not."* Somebody is thankful for the second part of this verse because he or she is thinking, "I don't have anything to give." No, you have something. You just don't have it for God. God is not letting you off the hook. God will judge what you give, and God knows what you have because He gave it to you in the first place. God knows the talent that you have. God

*The strong are to bear the infirmities of the weak*

knows the time that you can make. God knows the money that you have. God knows. You say, "I don't have anything," yet you have big houses. You're driving big cars. You're wearing fine clothes. **You've got it, you just don't have it for God.** You are out of the will of God. God knows what you have and He judges. If we give willingly, it is accepted in relation to what we have, not what we do not have.

## Take Care of One Another Equally

The strong are to bear the infirmities of the weak (Rom. 15:1a). This verse says that we have to take care of one another, equally. As children of God, we have no choice but to take care of those who are unlikely, oppressed and downtrodden. Our budget should also reflect this. The church has to understand that the call of God is an unending call to missions. We have to learn to take care of our people and help our people learn to take care of themselves.

The church has to learn to deal with unemployment. I'm not just talking about the unemployed who are on the streets. We have people in our congregation right now, dressed up, sitting beside you and me who are unemployed. We have to deal with

> *We've got to do some trickle-down grace, some trickle-down blessings and some trickle-down spirit.*

problems like no skills. You can't get a job today without marketable skills. They can't type. They don't know how to use a computer. Somebody has to train people how to use a computer.

Somebody's got to catch the spirit. We've got to do some trickle-down grace, some trickle-down blessings and some trickle-down spirit. I still have my white waiter's coat, if my wife hasn't thrown it away. I've kept it because I believe that if I don't have any other kind of job, I can get a job waiting tables. As a waiter, God prepared me to pastor. Somehow we have to prepare our people. We have to deal with holistic ministry. God wants us to minister to every part of His creation. He wants us to minister not only to their souls, but also to their minds, income and marketability.

## Summary

We have an unending call to missions. Maybe if we answer, then the church next door will answer too. Somebody has to get it started. The only thing I know is that a dying world needs to see Jesus in the churches. The church is the physical body of Christ to a sick, dying and greedy world. Jesus is not in the flesh running up and down the streets. Perhaps if we answer God's call, our children will be able to say that there were people who heard the Word of God, caught the Spirit of God and abounded in the grace of giving.

**Exodus 4:1–2**

[1]And Moses answered and said, But, behold, they will not believe me, nor hearken unto my voice: for they will say, The LORD hath not appeared unto thee. [2]And the LORD said unto him, What *is* that in thine hand? And he said, A rod.

**Matthew 25:14–30 (NIV)**

[14]Again, it will be like a man going on a journey, who called his servants and entrusted his property to them. [15]To one he gave five talents of money, to another two talents, and to another one talent, each according to his ability. Then he went on his journey. [16]The man who had received the five talents went at once and put his money to work and gained five more. [17]So also, the one with the two talents gained two more. [18]But the man who had received the one talent went off, dug a hole in the ground and hid his master's money. [19]After a long time the master of those servants returned and settled accounts with them. [20]The man who had received the five talents brought the other five. "Master" he said, "you entrusted me with five talents. See, I have gained five more." [21]His master replied, "Well done, good and faithful servant! You have been faithful with a few things; I will put you in charge of many things. Come and share your master's happiness!"

*continued on page 140*

**Matthew 25:14–30 (NIV) continued**

²²The man with the two talents also came. "Master," he said, "you entrusted me with two talents; see, I have gained two more." ²³His master replied, "Well done, good and faithful servant! You have been faithful with a few things; I will put you in charge of many things. Come and share your master's happiness!" ²⁴Then the man who had received the one talent came. "Master" he said, "I knew that you are a hard man, harvesting where you have not sown and gathering where you have not scattered seed. ²⁵So I was afraid and went out and hid your talent in the ground. See, here is what belongs to you." ²⁶His master replied, "You wicked, lazy servant! So you knew that I harvest where I have not sown and gather where I have not scattered seed? ²⁷Well then, you should have put my money on deposit with the bankers, so that when I returned I would have received it back with interest. ²⁸Take the talent from him and give it to the one who has the ten talents. ²⁹For everyone who has will be given more, and he will have an abundance. Whoever does not have, even what he has will be taken from him. ³⁰And throw that worthless servant outside, into the darkness, where there will be weeping and gnashing of teeth."

# What's That in Your Hand?

## The Stewardship of Talents

A wealthy man, a man of much wisdom was once asked the question, What's the most serious thought that has ever entered your mind? Without hesitation he said, "The most serious thought that ever entered my mind was, What is my responsibility to God?" What is our Christian responsibility to God? I think that is a good question. Jesus gives us the answer in a parable. A parable is a life situation that has great spiritual truths. Seemingly, we learn better, quicker and more in depth from experience. Jesus invites us on an experiential journey in and through this parable on the stewardship of talents, a parable that has great spiritual truths.

Before we begin our journey, I want to lift up four propositions that hopefully and prayerfully will bring meaning and maybe even some conviction in your heart along the way.

1. A Christian steward is called to live in courageous faith; not just faith, but courageous faith.

2. A talent is different than a gift and we all have more than one talent.

3. God approves of the church investing her money.

4. God is not interested in what you don't have.

Come go with me on an experiential journey through the parable of the talents and let God instruct us on these propositions.

## The Parable of the Talents

The Bible begins the parable by saying that a certain man was going on a journey and he called some servants together and entrusted his property to them. Keep in mind that the certain man is God. We are the servants. We need to understand that as this parable unfolds, the talents never belonged to the servants. God is the owner. That's what stewardship is about. A steward is one to whom God has entrusted something. The steward doesn't own it. He manages it. God has given us His creation so we ought to be good stewards of it.

The man called the three servants together and made them stewards. He gave five talents to one, two talents to the second and one talent to the third. The Bible says He gave the talents according to their ability (Matt 25:15b). He knew the servant to whom he gave one talent wasn't going to do anything with it from the start. Some of us are not ready for a blessing. God knows that we don't have the ability to receive a big blessing.

To make this more meaningful, we need to turn these talents into money. I like the way the New International Version says "talents of money" (Matt. 25:15). During those times, a talent was converted into an amount by using silver and gold as the standard of measure. Let's say that one talent was worth $10,000. So he gave one servant $50,000 to hold for him. He gave the second servant $20,000 and the third $10,000, all according to their ability.

He then took his trip. When he returned, He wanted to know what they had done with the money he had entrusted to them. The man with the $50,000 said, "Lord, here is your $50,000 and $50,000 more. I invested your money. I did something with it"

(Matt. 25:20). God said, "You good and faithful servant! You have been faithful over a few things and now I will place you in charge of many things. Enter into the joys of your reward. Enter into the happiness of God" (Matt. 25:21). He said the same to the servant to whom he had given $20,000 and who now had $40,000.

Then came the servant with the $10,000. He said, "Lord I knew you were a hard man. So I put your money in a hole and here it is" (Matt. 25:24–26). God said, "You wicked, lazy servant. As a matter of fact, take that $10,000 and give it to the boy who has $100,000" (Matt. 25:26a, 28). Then God cast him into the outer rim of darkness. God cast him into the outer rim of rewards. He took the stars out of his crown. He took all of the rewards from him. The Bible says that there was weeping and gnashing of teeth (Matt. 25:30b).

> *Often, we are so much in the "give me" mode that we get out of the giving mode.*

## What's That in Your Hand?

Often, we are so much in the "give me" mode that we get out of the giving mode. Do you have children? If so, you will frequently hear them say "give me." Some times they go a little fast and they say "gimme." Gimme, gimme, gimme will make you sick. History tells us that Rockefeller was a sick, pitiful man until he was blessed with the grace of giving.

God is asking us today, "What's that in your hand? Have I provided you with any opportunities? Have I put you in a position of influence in your community?" God is asking each of us individually, "Didn't I bless you? Didn't I give you a voice to sing? Why aren't you in the choir? Haven't I given you a mind to think? Why aren't you working in Fulfillment Hour (Sunday School)? Haven't I given you a job? Why aren't you tithing my money? Have I kept you alive? Why aren't you serving me? Have I loved you? Why don't you prove the sincerity of your love? Didn't I save you? Why don't you help others get saved? What's that in your hand?"

Like Moses, we excuse ourselves by making appeals to God based on what we don't have. We say I'm too old, too young, too educated, too poor, not good enough, not good-looking enough, and not smart enough. When God told Moses to go and tell Pharaoh, *"Let my people go"* (Ex. 5:1), Moses said, "Who am I that I might go? They won't believe me. I'm not eloquent. My speech is slow when I talk." But God said to Moses, "What's that in your hand?" The same question He asked Moses, He's asking the members of the church collectively and individually, "What talents have I given you? What's that in your hand?" **God calls us to live in courageous faith, not just faith; but courageous faith.** He wants us to believe that we can do anything He has called us to do. God is not interested in what we don't have. He's interested in using what we already have in our hands.

## One-Talent Christians

I think as we take this biblical journey, we can vividly see that many of us are one-talent Christians. We act like that one-talent Christian in the parable. Instead of being an adventure, our faith becomes a chain of obligation. We cling to the status quo, hoping that we can get by without a crisis or challenge. We are content with the usual routine of the life of the church, always doing everything the same way. We don't want the church to venture too far.

*God is not interested in what we don't have. He's interested in using what we already have in our hands.*

The one-talent Christian fails to see how much he or she is needed and the result is stewardship without a sail, like a ship without a sail. A ship without a sail goes nowhere. Stewardship without a sail does nothing. We need to put some wind in our stewardship sail.

Often, we think a talent is a spiritual gift and that we have only one. I submit to you that everything we have is comprised of a talent God entrusted to us. This includes all of the abilities and capabilities we use every minute of the day. It includes our material and financial resources as well as our relationships with our loved ones and friends. Yes, there is a stewardship of relationships with loved ones and friends. It also includes our influence at church, on our jobs and in the community. It even includes our gift of salvation. God saved us and we ought to be good stewards of His gift of salvation. In short, our stewardship includes our very lives.

*Christian stewardship is the proper management of God-owned resources.*

## Managing God-Owned Resources

Christian stewardship is the proper management of God-owned resources. Adam and Eve were in the Garden of Eden for one purpose and that was to take care of God's garden. God owned the garden, but Satan convinced Adam and Eve that it was their garden. The very first sin in this creation was over ownership. It is the sin that caused all of these other sins that would condemn us, if it had not been for Jesus. All of these other sins have us sick and messed up in this ill world. People killing each other, carjacking, sex being misused on TV, people cursing and doing everything they can imagine. It all began with the sin of ownership.

The only way we'll get back to what God intended for us is to rebuke Satan. Satan told Adam and Eve not to listen to God. He told them, "This could be your garden. That could be your tree. That could be your fruit. Do what you want to do in the garden." The voice of Satan is still heard today. "Go ahead! Spend! Forget about what the Bible says. Forget about what that preacher is preaching. Spend it the way you want. It's yours. You earned it. You worked for it. You deserve it." Have you heard the voice of Satan recently? I know I have, but if you're like me, you have to rebuke Satan. Talk back to Satan. Tell him, "Satan, get thee behind me. This is God's money. These are God's resources. He entrusted me with them and you can't have them Satan."

*The very first sin in this creation was over ownership.*

## God Wants His Wealth Invested

God wants His wealth invested. He is not pleased when we hoard or accumulate what He intended to be invested and circulated. God's creative order is designed in a giving disposition. When we change from a giving disposition to a getting disposition, we go against the

*God approves of the church investing her money.*

nature of creation and contradict the nature of God. John 3:16 says, *"God so loved the world that he **gave** His only begotten son."*

God approves of the church investing her money. There may be a question of how to invest it, what to invest in and when to invest, but there is not a question of if the church should invest nor is there a question of either/or. God approves of the church investing her money. The power of God is placed in us, the people of God. It is an investment in others. The problem, I think, is when we hear the term *bank* our minds immediately go into secular thinking because bank is a secular term.

## We are Accountable for Our Talents

We are accountable to God for our talents. God is coming back and He's holding us accountable for what we keep, spend and give back. God holds us responsible for the 90 percent we keep and what we do with it, not just the 10 percent we give to Him. In other words, although you may be giving your tithe of a tenth, it's time to move up to another level. When you go before the throne of grace, you can't say, "I tithed, Lord." He said this you ought to do to show love, mercy and joy.

God holds us accountable for our relationships, influence and our lives. All that He has given us belongs to God. He told the two faithful servants, "Come up a little higher and I'll make you rulers over many things. Enter now into the joys of your rewards." He told the unfaithful one, "You are a bad child. I will take the star from your crown. I will take away your rewards."

The Bible says not only was there gnashing of teeth, but also crying. They put him some place where a whole lot of folks were crying. So he wasn't the only one. You know how badly you feel when something is taken from you. You cry. God put him outside of the blessing room and into the place of darkness where there was crying.

## Summary

God took the one talent and gave it to the one who had ten talents. He took the $10,000 and gave it to the one who had $100,000. The spiritual truth that we learn here is: Use it or lose it. God will take your

*Use it or lose it.*

beautiful singing voice, give it to me, and leave you wondering how I got it when you will have given it to me. Everything we have belongs to God and He's holding us accountable for properly managing His resources. How are you using your talents? God is asking, "What's that in your hand?"

**Haggai 1:5–7**

[5]Now therefore thus saith the LORD of hosts; Consider your ways. [6]Ye have sown much, and bring in little; ye eat, but ye have not enough; ye drink, but ye are not filled with drink; ye clothe you, but there is none warm; and he that earneth wages earneth wages *to put it* into a bag with holes. [7]Thus saith the LORD of hosts; Consider your ways.

# Consider Thy Ways

Biblical giving results in a harvest of blessings. Notice, I said "biblical" giving; not just giving according to our own understanding, but right giving, correct giving according to the Word of God. The purpose of this message is to teach us the way God wants us to give. God's way will result in a harvest of blessings. God says to us, consider your ways.

God says you have sown much, but you bring in little. You eat, yet you're still hungry. You drink, but you're still thirsty. You wear fine, warm clothes, yet you're cold and there is some void in your life. You work

*Biblical giving results in a harvest of blessings.*

everyday and still have nothing while living from paycheck to paycheck. You earn money, but you put it in bags that have holes in them. Something is wrong with this picture. Consider your ways. You might need a new bag of attitude or a new bag of thinking. Maybe you need a new bag of instructions or guidelines. If you are working everyday and still living from paycheck to paycheck, you need to check yourself out. You need to consider your ways.

Some of you have been working hard since you were eighteen or twenty-one years old and you don't have anything in the bank. There are others, and the scripture speaks to you, who have a whole lot in the bank. You have CD's, e-trade and Merrill Lynch. You clicked on Ameritrade and bought some UPS stock in the IPO section. It went up to $75. You sold it and you still are not satisfied. You still can't give God praise. There is still a void in your life. You are materially rich, but spiritually bankrupt. Consider your ways.

## The Israelite Example

We know that Moses built the tabernacle (temple) before the exile. He called for the people to bring money, silver and gold to build the tabernacle. The people brought so much that Pastor Moses had to say, "That's enough. You're bringing too much" (Ex. 36:5–7). Later, the tabernacle was destroyed and Solomon built a real temple for God. During the exile, that temple was also destroyed as the called out people of God, the ecclesia (the church of the Old Testament), was marched into Babylon for seventy years because of their sins.

In Babylon, they sat by the river Kebar wondering how they could sing a new song in a strange land. Then, God set them free and they went home to Jerusalem. They started rebuilding the temple under the leadership of Haggai and Zechariah. As they built, they became discouraged along the way. Haggai talked to them about their situation. The Lord had brought them out of Egypt, out of bondage. The Lord had opened up the Red Sea before them. The Lord had helped them fight the Battle of Jericho. He had helped them overcome the Ammorites, Malachites and Moabites. He had won all their battles for them. The Lord had led them across the Jordan into the land of milk and honey. He had even led them out of captivity again, out of northern Babylon. Now he had brought them back to Jerusalem and Judea. He had even let them build luxurious homes. Yet, the temple, God's church, stood in ruins.

It wasn't that they didn't have money. Haggai told them, "You are working good jobs. God has set you free. Now you are back at home in Jerusalem and we need to finish the work that was begun. You have good jobs, yet you bring in little. You're eating, yet you are still hungry. You are drinking but there is no drink in God's house. Something is wrong" (Hag. 1:5–7).

Here we are some 10,000 years later and not a whole lot has changed. God has begun a good work in us. Yet, some of us have good jobs but bring in little. Some of us are eating fine, but still have voids in our souls. We're wearing fine clothes to church, but putting very little in the offering tray. God says that something is wrong. The New Testament asks, *"What profit is it to a man if he gains the whole world, and loses his own soul?" (Matt. 16:26 NKJV).*

> *The problem is that many of us are giving according to our own understanding and not giving according to the Word of God or scripture.*

## No Tipping

The problem is that many of us are giving according to our own understanding and not giving according to the Word of God. Giving according to our understanding results in tipping God on Sunday mornings rather than tithing to Him. I believe that we need to put up a sign in the church that says "NO TIPPING."

When eating in a restaurant, we are supposed to tip the waiter of our table. We need to understand that God is not our waiter. He is the provider of our table. God is not waiting on our table. He provides the table, everything that is on it and everything that is in it. When we eat at that restaurant, He provides the waiter, the fork and the food. It all comes from God. We tip the waiter, but we tithe to the provider. Consider your ways.

*We tip the waiter, but we tithe to the provider.*

## You Can't Beat God Giving

Do you believe that you can't beat God giving? Your arms are too short. Your heart is too hard. Your love is too shallow. Your mercy is too temporary. Your grace is too insufficient. Everything you do is too legalistic. Your thoughts are too restricted. You can't beat God giving. His arms are too long. His hands are too big. His grace is too sufficient. His love is too unconditional and His mercy is everlasting to everlasting.

You can't beat God giving no matter how you try. It is a spiritual law that is supported by scripture and it is as real as the law of gravity. Most of us believe in the law of gravity. It simply says that what goes up, must come down. I am sure that we all believe the law of what goes up, must come down. The law of "you can't beat God giving" (no matter how you try) is just as real, true, meaningful, authentic and authoritative.

There are several points we should understand about the law of "you can't beat God giving":

1. **We cannot negotiate with God, yet God *can* negotiate with us.** Some of us think that we can negotiate with God. We want to say, "God I will give my tithe, if you do this." Our hearts are too hard. Our love is too shallow. We can't negotiate with God because we are too weak and frail. Yet, God can negotiate with us and He does. He says, "Try me and see if I won't pour out a blessing you can't hold." It is like He draws a line in the sand and says, "I dare you to step across it." On our side of the line is reason and logic. On God's side of the line is faith. God is saying, "Step out of reason and into faith. Then, see if I won't open the windows of heaven. Try me. Prove me."

2. **You reap what you sow (Gal. 6:7).** If we sow little, we will reap little. The Bible says that whatever measure you use in your giving, the same measure will be used in the return (Luke 6:38). This might answer the question that

everybody keeps putting to me about the "net" and the "gross." I am asked, "Should I tithe on my net earnings or my gross earnings?" Forget about this matter of your "take home pay." I think you have a legitimate question when you talk about before taxes or after taxes, but you don't have a legitimate question when you talk about your take home pay.

Some of you think your net is what you have left after the credit union has taken out your car note, your annuity and another loan you have, and then you say, "That's my net pay." That is what we call "take home pay." It is not your net. There is a whole lot of difference between net and take home. If you want to receive netly, then tithe netly. If you want to receive grossly, then tithe grossly.

It is not only the amount we sow, but also what we sow. If we sow corn, we will get corn. If we sow bad things, we will get bad things. We can't help somebody without helping ourselves. We can't hurt anybody without hurting ourselves. George Washington Carver said that in order to throw a man in a ditch, you have to get in the ditch with him.

3. **If you hold on too tightly, you can and lose everything.** God really doesn't need you to tithe. He has different ways of getting it. You might not bring it to the church, but He might send a doctor to the church who is a tither, and then send you to the doctor. He might send an undertaker to the church who is a tither, and then send you to the undertaker. The undertaker can bring your tithe. God works in mysterious ways. He will get His because He has all power.

4. **Sometimes God returns our blessings in material things, but He always returns them in spiritual things.** Have you ever gone to your mailbox and found a check that you didn't know was coming? Have you

*Where there is a spiritual action, there will be a spiritual reaction.*

picked up the phone and the caller said he had taken care of your car note? Sometimes God blesses us that way, but He blesses us spiritually all of the time. That's guaranteed! The writer of Proverbs says that a liberal man's soul is made fat and his heart is enlarged" (Prov.11:25).

That is the law of "you can't beat God giving." It operates on another law that is known in biblical circles as the law of "spiritual action and reaction."

## Spiritual Action and Reaction

Where there is a spiritual action, there will be a spiritual reaction. In Proverbs 3:9–10, it says:

*"Honour the LORD with thy substance, and with the firstfruits of all thine increase...so shall thy barns be filled with plenty, and thy presses shall burst out with new wine."*

We must give our firstfruits. To give our firstfruits is a spiritual action. God's pouring out of the blessing is a spiritual reaction. Malachi 3:10 says, *"Bring ye all of the tithes into... mine house."* It does not say United Way, Boy Scouts or any other benevolent organizations. He says bring it into mine house. That is a spiritual action. Then the scripture says:

*"Prove me now herewith...if I will not open you the windows of heaven and pour you out a blessing that there shall not be room enough to receive it."*

That is the spiritual reaction. Luke 6:36 teaches us that if we give, we will get. Giving is a spiritual action. Getting is a spiritual reaction. Notice that I said *spiritual* action. I did not say an action of the *flesh*, nor did I say a *human* action. A spiritual action means that it is given in the true spirit of God. Galatians 6:8 says that if we give for the wrong reasons, we will reap bad things. That is the key to this spiritual formula. Our motives must be right! God loves a cheerful giver. Therefore, it is not for me or anyone else to tell you how much to give. Don't force anyone to give anything he or she doesn't want to give. It won't do any good anyway because God loves a cheerful giver. The action must be a spiritual action. Then you will experience a spiritual reaction.

## Gnosticism

I know we have problems with that. Our problem is not new. They had a similar problem in all of Paul's churches in Asia Minor. Whether it was the church at Corinth, Ephesus, Philippi or Thessalonica, gnosticism was always creeping into the church. Gnosticism exists today. What is gnosticism? It is a special knowledge of the spirit(ual). Some people think they have a special knowledge that enables them to separate the spirit(ual) from reality. It is like a young man saying to his bride-to-be, "We are not going to deal with this real stuff. We are not going to a real preacher for marriage. We are not going to get a real license. We are not going to get a real bank account together. We are not going to buy a real house. We are not going to sleep in a real bed. We are not going to make real love. Honey, I will just love you in the spirit." What do you think that bride would say?

The church is Jesus' bride. There are folks who are saying that I'm not going to get in a real car on Sunday morning, drive on a real highway, go into a real sanctuary, go to a real Fulfillment Hour (Sunday School) class, sit down with real people or give real money. Lord, I'm just going to love you in the spirit! There are Gnostics in our church today who try to have a special knowledge of the Holy Spirit and think they can separate the Holy Spirit from reality. God says, "Shame on you. Consider your ways."

## Summary

Consider your ways. Are you full, yet empty? Are you eating, yet hungry? Are you drinking, yet thirsty? Are you prosperous, yet poor? There is a God hole in all of us. He made us that way. The only way we can fill that God hole is with God. We can't fill it with money in the bank. We can't fill it with a bottle of whiskey. We can't fill it with sex. We can't fill it with crack cocaine. We can't fill it with prestige. We can't fill it with power. We can't fill it with new cars. We can't fill it with new houses. We can't fill it with new clothes. The only way we can fill the God hole in us is with God Himself.

Are you full of Jesus? Are you filled with the Holy Spirit? Have you made Jesus Lord of your life? Is He Lord of your house? Is He Lord of your money? Are you giving according to God's principles? Are you giving the firstfruits? Are you giving purposefully? Are you giving willingly? Are you giving sacrificially? Are you tipping God or tithing to Him? Consider your ways and think on this: Jesus is the firstfruit. He gave Himself first. He is also the firstfruit of the resurrection. He arose first and gave us the promise of a resurrected body. Think it over and consider your ways.

# Part Two:


# God's Progressive Giving Plan

# An Overview of God's Progressive Giving Plan

God's Progressive Giving Plan provides the infrastructure for raising faith vs. raising money. This prototype has been used at the Greenforest Community Baptist Church where I pastor for the past twenty-three years. In that time, our contributions have grown from $13,000 to $5,000,000 ($5 million) a year. A prototype is a tried and proven method that can be packaged and duplicated. I firmly believe that this plan can be duplicated in other churches. The results may be greater or lesser depending on many factors. However, be assured that the results will be greater than if this plan or no plan was implemented. A church that fails to implement a planned approach to giving will never reach its God-given potential and lag pitifully behind in its stewardship. For all practical purposes, any plan is better than no plan. People do not plan to fail. They fail to plan. Also, keep in mind that a prototype is to be followed step by step to assure the best results. Some things may not fit well in your church setting. Some things may need fine tuning, but changes in the step-by-step procedure should be made *only after the initial process has been given an opportunity to fail* and after careful consideration.

God's Progressive Giving Plan advocates the biblical mandate to grow. Growing in Christ includes growing in giving. Grace, not law, is the foundational premise upon which God's Progressive Giving Plan is built. Therefore, the tithe is not taught from a legalistic perspective, but rather as a biblical principle and standard (review the chapter entitled "The Biblical Principle of the Tithe: God's Standard for Giving"). God's Progressive Giving Plan leads and encourages its participants to give far beyond the tithe. Also, because of the foundational premise of grace, the participants are allowed to grow into becoming tithers. Some believers have criticized this approach because it permits a Christian to give less than 10 percent as they grow into tithing. God's Progressive Giving Plan simply meets believers at their current level of existence. Jesus always met people where they were. For example, He met the Samaritan woman at her level of existence, living with a man who was not her husband. Yet, Jesus transformed her into an evangelist shouting, "Come see a man!" Historically, most participants in the plan are tithers or people who contribute above the standard 10 percent.

Although, God's Progressive Giving Plan permits believers to give less than 10 percent as they grow to become tithers, the plan's success requires strict obedience to all of the other major principles of giving that are taught in the Bible:

- Firstfruit giving
- Purposeful giving
- Willful giving
- Sacrificial giving

## Organizational Structure and Administrative Roles

A general Stewardship Ministry administers God's Progressive Giving Plan. The Stewardship Ministry functions throughout the year and is responsible for the fiscal (financial) affairs of the church.

The Stewardship Ministry's responsibilities include:

- Counting the collections
- Making the bank deposits
- Preparing the budget
- Monitoring expenditures and cash flow
- Teaching the congregation to apply biblical principles of financial management to their personal finances
- Promoting stewardship (all year)
- Coordinating Stewardship Emphasis month

The Stewardship Ministry is directed by a chairperson and should include the church's treasurer and/or business manager, a financial secretary and at least seven to ten other persons.

God's Progressive Giving Plan is most effective when it is understood that the pastor is the leader and chief administrator. The pastor's leadership style will determine the pastor's level of involvement. The Stewardship Ministry is composed of three divisions:

- Budget and Accounting
- Education and Promotion
- Counting

The Budget and Accounting Division is responsible for the budget-making phase of the budgetary process. The Education and Promotional Division is responsible for the budget-raising phase. The Counting Division counts each Sunday's collections and makes the bank deposits.

The following organizational chart on the following page illustrates the organizational structure and lists the primary responsibilities of each division.

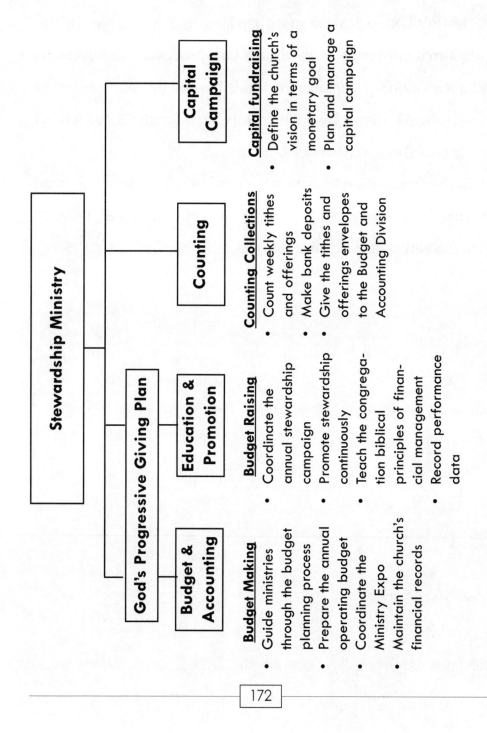

**Stewardship Ministry**

**God's Progressive Giving Plan**

**Budget & Accounting**

**Budget Making**
- Guide ministries through the budget planning process
- Prepare the annual operating budget
- Coordinate the Ministry Expo
- Maintain the church's financial records

**Education & Promotion**

**Budget Raising**
- Coordinate the annual stewardship campaign
- Promote stewardship continuously
- Teach the congregation biblical principles of financial management
- Record performance data

**Counting**

**Counting Collections**
- Count weekly tithes and offerings
- Make bank deposits
- Give the tithes and offerings envelopes to the Budget and Accounting Division

**Capital Campaign**

**Capital fundraising**
- Define the church's vision in terms of a monetary goal
- Plan and manage a capital campaign

## Budget Making and Budget Raising

God's Progressive Giving Plan has two concurrent, but separate processes—budget making and budget raising. The success of each process depends on the effectiveness of both. Budget making addresses the administrative and accounting aspects of planning, organizing and producing a budget to be reviewed and approved by the entire congregation. A budget is a written, projected plan of income and expenditures for a given period of time, usually a year.

Budget raising addresses the issue of how the money will be obtained to fulfill the projected budget. In God's Progressive Giving Plan, traditional selling to raise money for the budget is not advocated. The only biblical way to raise the budget is through tithes and offerings. Hence, our aim is to raise the level of giving through tithes and offerings. For the purpose of clarity, we will discuss budget making and raising separately in the following chapters.

## Counting Division

The Counting Division counts the weekly collections and makes the bank deposits. I recommend involving as many people as possible in this process. It is best if different counters work at least one Sunday each month. This helps to foster an environment of trust. It also gives more members an opportunity to see the level of giving. However, at least two trained Lead Counters should be present each Sunday.

The counters should be rotated ever year. This prevents anyone from becoming burned-out and it allows new members the opportunity to become actively involved in the Stewardship Ministry. All new counters should be trained by an experienced counter.

The Counting Division is only responsible for counting. They do not record any data except to tally the amounts received. They are to indicate the amounts collected for the operating budget and the capital campaign separately, and then prepare the bank deposits.

Numbered envelopes should be used to identify each member or family unit. The counters give the empty envelopes to the Financial Secretary who records the data from the envelopes into the church's financial recordkeeping system. The Financial Secretary is a member of the Budget and Accounting

Division and is responsible for issuing quarterly giving statements to the members.

When selecting an envelope system, you can have one envelope with separate lines for the operating budget (tithes and offerings) and the capital campaign or you can have two separate envelopes—one for tithes and offerings and another for capital campaign contributions. Having one envelope with two separate lines makes it convenient for the members to write one check. Having two separate envelopes makes it easier for the counters to separate the monies. Regardless of the system you choose, the operating and capital funds must be kept separate.

# Budget Making

The Budget and Accounting Division is responsible for the budget-making phase. There are four goals or milestones in the budget-making process:

1. Request budgets from all ministries and auxiliaries.
2. Educate the ministry leaders to the principles and processes of God's Progressive Giving Plan.
3. Prepare a recommended operating budget for discussion with the leaders.
4. Prepare the proposed operating budget to be presented to the congregation for approval.

The budget-making process is undergirded by five factors:

1. Commitment to a ministry-driven budget rather than a maintenance-driven budget

2. Commitment to a unified budget

3. Commitment to inclusion (involving as many people as possible in the budget planning process)

4. Commitment to full disclosure

5. Leadership empowerment

## Ministry-Driven Budgets vs. Maintenance-Driven Budgets

God gives every church a mission. Each church is called to fulfill a specific place and function within the body of Christ. When a church recognizes and accepts its calling, God will send the people to carry out His ministry. The church must discern how to effectively fulfill God's purposes through its ministry, people and resources.

The budget gives expression to the church's ministry over a specific period of time. It is a means of unifying and supporting the church's ministries to do what God wants them to do. The budget should reflect the church's ministry, not just in numbers but also in worship, witnessing, growth and reaching out to a world of people who are in need of Christ. Therefore, the church's budget should be a ministry-driven budget.

Ministry-driven budgets are based on prayer and discernment of God's will relative to the life of the church for the coming year. Maintenance-driven budgets are based on satisfying the status quo. Ministry-driven budgets are founded on faith. Maintenance-driven budgets are established by sight. God calls us to walk by faith, not by sight. Therefore, a ministry-driven budget is biblical while a maintenance-driven budget is unbiblical. If a budget is ministry-driven (biblical), it will always be more than the actual income of the previous year. Being ministry-driven is absolutely essential to the success of the budget-making process.

## Unified Budget

The budget should not only be ministry-driven, it should also be "unified." A *unified budget* is a budget where all money is accounted for and managed under one budget. The individual ministries and auxiliaries such as ushers and choirs are **not** permitted to have independent, separate bank accounts. A unified budget facilitates management and goes a long way toward dispelling notions and perceptions of dishonesty. Separate bank accounts open the door for rumors, misappropri ations and mishandling of money. They also facilitate dishonesty.

The ministries and auxiliaries are allocated *auxiliary budgets*. The auxiliary budgets are justified in accordance with the ministry's mission statement and the church's vision. The dollars for approved line items are held within the unified budget. The ministry/auxiliary submits requests to the unified budget for all expenditures. Requests are authorized for approved line items only. The ministry/auxiliary is expected to manage its spending within its approved budget.

## Inclusion

The more involvement in the budget planning process, the more members take ownership of the values, purposes and vision of the church. The more ownership there is of the vision, the higher the level of giving. Too often the only folks involved in the budgetary process is a small, exclusive number of people, such as the church treasurer or financial officer. Limiting the number of people in the budget-making process defeats the purpose of this approach to stewardship. Inclusive involvement increases giving, exclusive involvement decreases giving.

## Full Disclosure

Full disclosure means informing the congregation in a user-friendly manner of all information regarding the budget. This stewardship approach calls for every member to be informed of every penny taken in and every penny spent. Informed congregations who own and value the purpose and vision of the church give more than uninformed congregations.

## Leadership Empowerment

To empower means to give authority or power to carry out a task or responsibility. Once the budget has been approved or ratified, ministry and auxiliary leaders must be allowed to manage their individual line items. After the budget has been approved, monitoring is needed to assure that all requests are indeed approved budgeted items and that cash flow is adequate.

Empowerment eliminates confusion and conflict during the year. Confusion and conflict stifle giving. Harmony encourages giving. Leadership empowerment promotes harmony and thereby increases giving.

# Budget Raising

A budget without money is meaningless. Sometimes church members think money is available because they see money in the budget that has not been spent. It would be wise to teach and remind members that a budget is only a financial projection to be used as a guide. Without actual money to support the budget, it is just useless paper. Therefore, raising money is absolutely necessary.

The Education and Promotion Division is responsible for the budget-raising phase. The major components of the budget-raising phase are:

1. Promotional campaign
2. Stewardship preaching and teaching revival
3. Sunday School and Bible Study lessons

4. Written commitments of percentage giving (equal sacrifice rather than equal gifts)

5. Testimonies

6. Performance data

7. Financial planning workshops

## Promotional Campaign

A campaign is an assertive and concerted effort to persuade people to think and vote in a particular way. Church members vote with their feet and their pocketbooks. The promotional campaign in God's Progressive Giving Plan is a consecrated stewardship effort to persuade believers to demonstrate their faith, love and thankfulness to God through biblical giving.

Campaigns are not unfamiliar to the church. Almost all churches at one time or another have participated in building campaigns. The major difference between this promotional campaign and the typical building campaign is that this one is shorter in duration. The time span for God's Progressive Giving Plan promotional campaign should be no more than one month. We refer to this period as Stewardship Emphasis Month.

It includes the following four promotional Sundays:

- **Acknowledgement Sunday:** Members acknowledge God as creator and owner of all things and their roles as stewards.

- **Prove the Tithe Sunday:** All members are encouraged to test the tithe by giving a tenth of their weekly income on this day.

- **Commitment Sunday:** All members are asked to turn in their written commitments by this day.

- **Victory Sunday:** The campaign results are announced and the congregation celebrates by giving thanks and honor to God for the great work He has done in and through them.

A fifth promotional Sunday, **Move Up Sunday**, is held the first Sunday of the next year when those who made commitments begin paying their tithes and offerings at the new levels they committed to during Stewardship Emphasis Month.

Like most campaigns, effective communication is essential. Communications strategies include letters to the congregation, banners, fliers, bulletin announcements, special envelopes, and essential pastoral communications from the pulpit. Lack of strong, effective communication from the pastor jeopardizes the campaign.

I encourage you to ask those members who have the gift of creative communication to assist the Stewardship Ministry in developing promotional activities. The Appendix contains the script for a stewardship skit that was written by Ms. Wanda Wynn, Director of the Drama Ministry at Greenforest Community Baptist Church. The skit, *Money Over Matters* is an example of what can be done when you involve other ministries of the church.

Remember to involve the children and youth. The Bible tells us to *"Train up a child in the way he should go: and when he is old, he will not depart from it" (Prov. 22:6)*. When children are taught the biblical principles of tithing and giving, they will grow into tithing and giving adults.

## Stewardship Preaching and Teaching Revival

The preaching of God's Word best persuades believers. Preaching is the most persuasive tool. The power of the pulpit is unsurpassed in the process of transformation. Therefore, preaching that includes teaching must be utilized in this budget-raising phase. This preaching must occur as the main sermon on each Sunday. God's Progressive Giving Plan calls for the senior pastor to preach at least three sermons on the general theme of "What the Bible Says About Giving" during the four promotional Sundays. Preaching about money is not popular, yet Jesus talked more about money than He did salvation. A special anointing is needed to preach effectively on money. Pastors should pray and ask God for this anointing. Preaching under this special anointing, I saw our actual contributions increase from $13,000 to $5,000,000 ($5 million) a year.

## Sunday School and Bible Study Lessons

Another important element of the teaching revival is Sunday School and Bible Study lessons on stewardship. We recommend that the same lesson be presented to all age groups—adults, children and youth. The materials would need to be appropriate for each age group, however the scripture text and message should be the same. If you are unable to find suitable prepared lessons, someone with the gift of teaching may be willing to write the lessons. Two adult lessons are included in the Appendix.

## Written Commitments

Commitments, not just commitments, but written commitments are a vital part of the budget-raising phase. God is a covenant God and we are a covenant people so we should not hesitate to be committed believers. Many believers commit to 30-year mortgages, car leases, credit cards and other high interest comforts, but rebel against committing any part of their lives to God. Here again, this approach to stewardship deals with spiritual growth. Raising one's faith to the level of commitment is faith raising, not money raising.

## Percentage Giving (Equal Sacrifices, Not Equal Gifts)

God's Progressive Giving Plan calls for all members to commit a specific percentage of their income as part of the budget-raising phase. Notice that it is very important that members are not asked to commit a certain dollar amount. Rather, they are encouraged to be obedient to the principles taught in the Bible by committing a designated percentage in adherence to the principles of first, purposeful, willing and sacrificial fruit. While definitely recognizing and honoring 10 percent as a tithe, the percentage committed may be more or less than 10 percent.

Members are asked, while in church, to use the Growth Giving Guide as a means of identifying their current level of giving. They are then asked to make a prayerful, purposeful decision to grow in percentage increments over at least the next five years. This approach to the stewardship of giving has proven to be very user-friendly. Since no specific dollar amount is requested, the only reason a believer would refuse to participate is that they possess a rebellious or disobedient spirit. The actual commitment card is on the reverse side of the Giving Growth Guide. (See the Appendix for a sample Giving Growth Guide & Commitment Card.)

## Testimonies

God has always been able to use a testimony. Testimonies are great tools for increasing the success of the budget-raising phase. History and experience have taught us that testimonies encourage others to try giving according to biblical principles and break materialistic strongholds. As a word of caution, testimonies should be limited to tithing and stewardship testimonies only, rather than general testimonies describing the overall goodness of God. If testimonies are not directed, members will give great testimonies, but unrelated to giving. Testimonies serve as water to prime the pump. There can be much water in the well, but if no one is willing to put some water in the pump as a primer, the water will remain in the well and unavailable. Likewise, there is much money in the possession of church members. Without testimonies to prime the congregation, the money may remain unavailable. The pastor and other church leaders should be the chief primers with their testimonies. The pastor, elders, deacons, trustees, ministers, ministry coordinators and chairpersons must lead with their testimonies. When the leadership fails to lead with their testimonies the budget-raising phase is greatly stifled.

It also helps to have a mixture of testimonies from different economic levels. The congregation needs to see people willing to give sacrificially from all walks of life.

## Performance Data

The first time you implement God's Progressive Giving Plan, you will not have any performance data except that which may be available through the history of your church's giving in previous years. However, once God's Progressive Giving Plan is implemented, every conceivable data relative to the church's giving, such as, the number of tithers, the number of written commitments, the growth record of the budget, etc., should be analyzed and archived. In future years, this data will be invaluable for promotional purposes and will add considerable credibility to the process.

Examples of the data that should be kept year-to-year are:

- Number of families
- Annual church budget
- Annual budget for each auxiliary
- Number of new commitments
- Number of recommitments
- Average income per household (as projected by the county's records)

I recommend tracking the campaign results by maintaining a spreadsheet that lists the number of commitments received at each percentage level from .5%–20% in half percent increments. This data should be recorded for each promotional Sunday and kept on a year-to-year basis. The spreadsheet should be given to the pastor as a weekly report during the campaign. See the "Commitment Tracking Form" in the Appendix for an example.

## Financial Planning Workshops

Financial Planning Workshops are used to teach the congregation how to apply God's principles for financial management to their personal finances. As stated earlier, money is often the last barrier that needs to be broken in many of our lives so that we can come into a full, right relationship with God. It is the stronghold that prevents God from being able to fully use many of us.

The financial planning workshops should be based on biblical principles and address the following issues:

- Family budgeting (money management)
- Debt reduction
- Estate planning

While information on the above topics is good to know, for the workshops to be truly effective, I recommend that practical assistance is provided in developing a workable family budget and debt-reduction plan and writing a will. These should be handled through confidential consultations with individuals who are qualified in personal finance and committed to practicing biblical financial management principles.

# Implementation Procedures

Prior to implementing God's Progressive Giving Plan, the church leadership should pray to discern God's will for their church and ask His guidance in implementing this program. Your church's leaders and the Stewardship Ministry should study this text and be thoroughly familiar with its principles so they can ensure that the program is carried out in a manner that is faithful to its design. Implementation should begin at least three to six months prior to the stewardship emphasis period because you will need time to select Spirit-filled leaders and educate them to their responsibilities and the processes of God's Progressive Giving Plan. You will also need an administrative infrastructure to support the program.

The implementation process includes these phases:

- Organizational
- Planning and Preparation
- Budget-Making
- Budget-Raising

During the organizational phase, Spirit-filled leaders are selected to fill the following positions:

- Stewardship Ministry Chairperson
- Church Treasurer or Business Manager
- Budget and Accounting Division (3–4 people)
- Education and Promotion Division (3–4 people)
- Counting Division (serving on a one-year rotational basis)

It is important that roles are well defined so that each division understands its function and the inter-dependencies that exist between the divisions.

The organizational phase is also the time to put the background processes in place that are needed to administer this program. Logistics need to be worked out for the following:

- Mailing list of all members
- Support to mail letters
- Database to identify committed and noncommitted

members. Depending on the size of your congregation, this may be a simple Microsoft® Excel spreadsheet or Access database or a sophisticated church membership and financial system.

- System for recording and archiving historical data for future use.

- Process for updating the membership records with new address information.

- Secure process for handling the commitment cards. The commitment cards will be placed in the offering trays. The counters will give the cards to the Education and Promotion Division who will record the campaign results, and then give the cards to the Financial Secretary (Budget and Accounting Division) for input into the database.

- Weekly reports to the pastor of the campaign results during Stewardship Emphasis Month.

- Tithing/offering envelopes that identify each contributor.

- Quarterly statements to individual members/families so they will have records of their giving for tax purposes.

- Monthly budget status provided to the congregation throughout the year.

## Planning and Preparation Phase

The purpose of the planning and preparation phase is to prepare for Stewardship Emphasis Month. This phase occurs at least one month prior to the start of the budget-making phase. The entire Stewardship Ministry should be involved in planning. The degree of involvement the pastor has will depend on his or her leadership style.

The key accomplishments during this phase are:

- Review the budget-making and budget-raising processes.
- Establish a date for budget approval. (All events will be driven by this date.)
- Develop a schedule of events for the Stewardship Emphasis Month that includes:
  - Leadership Workshop
  - Four promotional Sundays
  - Ministry Expo
  - Financial Planning Workshop(s)
- Define roles and delegate responsibilities.
- Plan the Leadership Workshop to explain the stewardship program to all ministry leaders.
- Draft letter to the ministry leaders requesting auxiliary budget submissions.

- Draft separate letters to noncommitted and previously committed members for the pastor's approval and signature. NOTE: If you do not have a record of previously committed tithers in the first year you implement God's Progressive Giving Plan, then send the same letter to everyone.

- Design commitment cards for the pastor's approval.

The Appendix contains planning tools and examples of memos, bulletin announcements, commitment cards, Sunday School lessons, etc. Feel free to reproduce any of these materials when carrying out your campaign.

The following describes the budget-making and budget-raising processes in God's Progressive Giving Plan. Remember these two processes occur concurrently and each is dependent on the other's success.

## Budget-Making Phase

The purpose of the budget-making phase is to develop the budget. The events that occur during the budget-making phase are driven by the date the budget will be approved.

The following is a step-by-step description of the budget-making process for God's Progressive Giving Plan:

**Step 1.** Approximately ten weeks before the budget is approved, the Budget and Accounting Division appeals to all committees and ministry leaders to submit their *auxiliary budget* requests for the coming year. The ministry leaders should be provided historical data that reflects the church's actual expenditures for the last year and the current year-to-date (with their line item highlighted). They should also be given a projection of their expenditures in the next year based upon their current spending rate. Finally, they should be provided budget worksheets for consistency and ease of consolidation. (See "Request for Auxiliary Budgets" in the Appendix.)

**Step 2**. Ministry leaders, coordinators and chairpersons enter into prayer, dialogue and meditation to discern God's will and the financial needs of their ministries.

**Step 3.** Eight weeks prior to budget approval, the Budget and Accounting Division conducts a Stewardship Leadership Workshop for all ministry leaders. Its purpose is to explain the key principles of God's Progressive Giving Plan, the budgetary process and the schedule of events. (See the Appendix for a bulletin announcement and an agenda.)

**Step 4.** Ministry leaders, coordinators and chairpersons turn in their *auxiliary budget* requests to the Budget and Accounting Division approximately six weeks before budget approval.

**Step 5.** The Budget and Accounting Division reviews each *auxiliary budget* request. It is very important that they do not judge or deny any request. They are to review each request in light of the vision of the church, the auxiliary's mission, past spending trends and patterns, the relationship of the request to the entire budget and the legitimacy of the ministry.

**Step 6.** The Budget and Accounting Division prepares a *recommended unified budget* to be discussed and decided upon in a budget planning meeting with all ministry leaders. The *recommended unified budget* includes line items for each auxiliary and the church's operating expenses. The *recommended unified budget* should list all of the auxiliary requests just as they were submitted with a separate column showing the recommended amount in light of the review. (See "Recommended Unified Budget" in the Appendix for an example.)

**Step 7.** Approximately four weeks before the budget is approved, the Budget and Accounting Division presents the *recommended unified budget* to all ministry leaders, coordinators and chairpersons in a budget planning meeting. The entire congregation is invited. The purpose of the meeting is to discuss and decide on the *recommended unified budget.* The outcome of this meeting is a *proposed unified budget,* possibly with a few minor revisions, that can be presented to the congregation for approval. (See "Budget Planning Meeting Announcement" in the Appendix.)

**Step 8.** Approximately three weeks before the *proposed unified budget* is approved, the Budget and Accounting Division sponsors a "Ministry Expo" where ministry leaders, coordinators and chairpersons present exhibits that explain their mission, strategy and budget's line items. The displays should be well thought out and tastefully decorated. The ministry leaders, coordinators, chairpersons and others responsible for managing any portion of the budget should be available at their exhibits to answer questions. (See examples of the "Ministry Expo Participation Appeal" and "Ministry Expo Announcement" in the Appendix.)

The expo should be planned well in advance so that facility support can be provided to all of the ministries. They will need assistance in obtaining tables, chairs, etc. Also, the cleanup afterwards should be a planned, coordinated effort.

**Step 9.** Approximately two weeks before the *proposed unified budget* is presented for approval, the Budget and Accounting Division distributes hard copies of the proposed budget to the entire congregation. (See "Proposed Unified Budget" in the Appendix.)

**Step 10**. Approximately four weeks before the end of the year, a meeting is held to approve the budget. (See "Budget Approval Meeting Announcement" in the Appendix.)

**Budget-Raising Phase**

The purpose of the budget-raising phase is to build the faith of the congregation so they will make financial commitments to raise the church's operating budget. This is accomplished primarily through anointed preaching of God's Word on the four promotional Sundays during Stewardship Emphasis Month. On these four Sundays, the pastor (or the appointed preacher) preaches messages related to stewardship. At least two of the messages should focus on the stewardship of money. Part One of this book contains inspirational messages that focus on stewardship and are directed at building faith. You are encouraged to preach these themes boldly under the anointing of the Holy Spirit. As the congregation grows in faith, the monetary contributions will increase beyond your expectation.

The following steps describe the budget-raising process of God's Progressive Giving Plan:

**Step 1.** Approximately six weeks before budget approval, the Education and Promotion Division mails a special letter to those members who have commitment cards on file from the previous year. The letter includes:

- Their previous commitment card
- A new commitment card and
- A self-addressed return envelope.

The letter should thank them mightily for their previous participation and encourage them to recommit by mail or in the next worship service. (See the Appendix for an example.)

**Step 2**. Approximately five weeks before the date the budget is to be approved, the Education and Promotion Division mails letters to the noncommitted members informing them of the upcoming stewardship campaign and encouraging them to participate. (See the Appendix for an example.)

**Step 3.** Approximately five weeks before the budget is approved, the Education and Promotion Division publishes the schedule of events for Stewardship Emphasis Month in the church's Sunday bulletin and other strategic locations throughout the church. (See "Stewardship Emphasis Schedule" in the Appendix.)

**Step 4.** The first Sunday of Stewardship Emphasis Month is "Acknowledgement Sunday." The purpose of this day is to acknowledge that God is creator, everything belongs to Him and we are His creation. Until believers acknowledge this relationship, we will never be good stewards. The pastor is to use his best leadership skills to promote the campaign by sharing his tithing/giving testimony and preaching a sermon on stewardship. Also, an appeal should be made for commitment cards. Remember, the commitment cards are the major success indicator used in raising the budget. The cards are important because they represent faith that translates into money. (See "Commitment Card" and "Giving Growth Guide" in the Appendix.)

**Step 5**. If you choose to present Bible Study lessons on stewardship, I recommend that they are taught during the week preceding "Prove the Tithe Sunday." This will help strengthen the congregation's willingness to "try the tithe."

**Step 6.** I recommend conducting the Financial Planning Workshop on the Saturday before "Prove the Tithe Sunday." The workshop is designed to show members how to follow God's principles when managing their money. The information they receive will help boost their courage to "try the tithe." (See "Financial Planning Workshop Announcement" in the Appendix.)

**Step 7.** The second Sunday of Stewardship Emphasis Month is "Prove the Tithe Sunday." On this Sunday, the entire congregation is encouraged to "try God" by giving the tithe. The Sunday School lessons on stewardship are presented to all age groups. (Two adult lessons are included in the Appendix.)

During worship, a stewardship sermon is preached, a testimony given and an appeal made for commitment cards. A special offering envelope may be used as a way of determining how many people chose to "prove the tithe."

**Step 8.** The third Sunday in Stewardship Emphasis Month is "Commitment Sunday." All commitment cards are due on this

Sunday. Again, a stewardship sermon is preached, a testimony given and an appeal made for commitment cards.

**Step 9.** The fourth Sunday of Stewardship Emphasis Month is "Victory Sunday." On this Sunday, the total number of commitments that were received and the total amount committed is announced to the congregation. God is given the glory and the church celebrates His victory in their giving.

**Step 10.** A "Thank You" notice is published in the bulletin on the first Sunday in December thanking the congregation for their support and participation. (See "Thank You Notice" in the Appendix.)

**Step 11.** "Move Up Sunday" is the first Sunday in the January of the next year. The congregation is reminded to "move up" to their new levels of giving. A copy of the approved budget is published in the bulletin. (See "Move Up Sunday Reminder" in the Appendix.)

# Part Three:

# Capital Stewardship

# Capital Stewardship Campaigns

The word campaign means a series of operations undertaken, generally using propaganda, to achieve a certain goal. Capital refers to the monetary resources needed to achieve the goal. Therefore, when we refer to a capital stewardship campaign we are speaking of a systematic, organized, series of events to promote the goal of raising money for a specific project, e.g., construction of a new facility or purchase of land.

The word campaign is often associated with political and military endeavors; therefore, some church members may perceive it as negative or secular. However, capital stewardship campaigns are indeed campaigns and require a lot of promotional communications if they are to be effective; all of which may be perceived as propaganda. The difference is that it is a spiritual campaign that is designed to promote a godly vision and further advance God's kingdom. In a sense money raising becomes the end and faith raising becomes the means.

The money raised in a capital campaign is always over and above the continuous, regular tithes and offering. Caution should be taken to prevent members from simply transferring money from their tithes and offerings to capital campaign projects. This is generally called robbing Peter to pay Paul. In other words, capital campaign contributions come from another pocket, and usually a deeper sacrificial pocket. Although, the goal is to raise money, if the campaign is based on God's word, and implemented in His Spirit, the church will experience a spiritual awakening and the level of faith will be raised.

The initial campaign usually takes place during a relatively short period of time, approximately six to eight weeks, excluding a preplanning period of four to six weeks. However, the objective is to solicit pledge contributions that are paid over a three-year period. So the life of the campaign is much longer. It is like a retail layaway plan, but the merchandise is a new facility or land.

The financial advantages of a capital campaign are tremendous. They include, but are not limited to:

- Making the facility affordable.
- Being debt free.
- Saving on interest (if a loan is required).

Most churches can expect to raise 2–2½ times their annual regular contributions.

## The Need for an Outside Consultant

One of the propositions that undergirds this book is that a separate procedure should be followed using an outside consultant to be effective in the stewardship of capital campaigns. I strongly recommend that a church not lean on its own understanding when implementing a capital campaign. Most pastors and churches have neither the time, expertise or focus required to conduct a successful capital campaign. Also, without an outside consultant and a proven systematic plan to follow, leaders will rely on previously learned methods and procedures that may not be biblically based. For example, many church leaders have learned to raise money for a building fund by asking for a predetermined dollar amount from each member.

This method is not equally sacrificial and therefore, is not biblical. Such a method is not promised to be blessed by God, and almost never results in a spiritual awakening or an increase in faith. Additionally, most capital campaigns attempted without an outside consultant do not result in the discovery of dormant spiritual gifts and talents. Such a discovery facilitates the spiritual awakening and raises faith.

Note, although an outside consultant is strongly recommended, knowledge of the campaign plan by the pastor and the support of the pastor is absolutely essential for success.

## Selecting an Outside Consultant

Choosing the right outside consultant for your church is critical. The right consultant for your church may or may not be the right consultant for another church. Each church has a unique profile; therefore, the outside consultant must be a right match.

When choosing an outside consulting firm, the integrity of the owner is of the utmost importance. In essence, the church is employing the services of a business whose owner is responsible for the total services rendered. After all other factors for selecting an outside consultant are considered, the integrity of the owner will be the most stable and reliable factor.

The list of criteria that should be considered when selecting an outside consultant include:

1. The consultant should be a Christian and possess a Christ-like spirit, demonstrated by past and present church activity and service.

2. The consultant should have a capital stewardship program that is biblical, based on God's principles for giving.

3. The consultant should have a proven record of implementing a successful capital campaign.

4. The consultant should have a practical knowledge of church dynamics that will allow him or her to relate to the pastor and other church leaders, as well as, anticipate actions and reactions from the general church membership.

5. The consultant should be culturally sensitive to the churches language and general way of doing church.

6. The consultant should be flexible, patient, have a sense of humor and possess a personality that matches the personality of your church.

7. The consultant should have leadership and project management skills that are evidenced by a successful track record, both as a consultant and in other past endeavors.

8. The consultant's fee should be affordable for the church's budget. Be aware that the consultant's fee is in addition to the cost of implementing the campaign.

## Counting the Cost

Another consideration in selecting an outside consultant is the cost. The Gospel of Luke cautions us to consider the cost before we begin building.

> *"For which of you, intending to build a tower, sitteth not down first, and counteth the cost, whether he have sufficient to finish it?" (Luke 14:28).*

Capital campaigns cost and outside consultants cost. The fact is, you have to spend money to raise money. Counting the cost mandates developing a budget. The budget needs to project both the cost of the consultant and the cost of implementing the campaign. The exact cost of implementing the campaign cannot be determined until after the consultant has been selected and the campaign plan has been developed.

The cost of the consultant is always negotiable. It is usually based on the size of your budget and/or the dollar amount you expect to raise. Commonly, the consultant's expenses are built into the final negotiated fee; therefore, you should not expect to be continuously billed for incidental costs, e.g., travel expenses or shipping of materials. Rather, you can expect to make predetermined payments with at least half of the total amount to be paid in the beginning.

Don't make the mistake of thinking less is better. Cheap is not necessarily best. You can make the mistake of spending too little for nothing. Give full consideration to the selection criteria in the above section. Be aware that the number one objection of the general congregation and leadership to using an outside consultant is the cost. Getting a consensus agreement from the leadership concerning cost is critical. Most consultants will make at least one free visit to the church to talk to the decision makers in an effort to secure your business. Don't hesitate to utilize this visit in the selection process.

Remember, once you have selected a consultant, try to follow his or her advice about implementing the campaign. You have agreed to pay for their expertise. It would not be good stewardship to spend money and not accept the services.

## Anointed Preaching

Another proposition on which this book is based is that the anointed preaching of God's Word is the best tool for stewardship transformation. Preaching is the most effective and successful way of delivering God's transforming Word. For the purpose of a working definition, preaching is defined as that which the preacher does that is labeled a sermon during the worship period regardless of content, style or form.

Never underestimate the power of the pulpit. Believers must hear what God wants them to know relative to money in sermonic fashion during the prime time Sunday hour. God tells us in Hosea 4:6, *"My people are destroyed for lack of knowledge."* Knowledge must be attained for faith to be raised.

The messages in the following section were preached during two successful capital campaigns—one that produced $1.5 million from a church that had annual regular contributions of $500,000 and another that raised $10 million from a church whose annual regular contributions were $5 million. I can personally bear witness that both campaigns resulted in a spiritual awakening, as spiritual gifts and talents were discovered and faith was raised.

# Capital Stewardship
# Messages

**Psalm 127:1–2**

¹Except the LORD build the house, they labour in vain that build it: except the LORD keep the city, the watchman waketh *but* in vain. ²*It is* vain for you to rise up early, to sit up late, to eat the bread of sorrows: for so he giveth his beloved sleep.

**Matthew 16:13–19**

¹³When Jesus came into the coasts of Caesarea Philippi, he asked his disciples, saying, Whom do men say that I the Son of man am? ¹⁴And they said, Some *say that thou* art John the Baptist: some, Elias; and others, Jeremias, or one of the prophets. ¹⁵He saith unto them, But whom say ye that I am? ¹⁶And Simon Peter answered and said, Thou art the Christ, the Son of the living God. ¹⁷And Jesus answered and said unto him, Blessed art thou, Simon Bar-jona: for flesh and blood hath not revealed *it* unto thee, but my Father which is in heaven. ¹⁸And I say also unto thee, That thou art Peter, and upon this rock I will build my church; and the gates of hell shall not prevail against it.

# Unless the Lord Builds the House

Sometime during the 60's, Aretha Franklin produced a song, maybe not as popular as some of her others, entitled *The House that Jack Built*. In this song she sang about how she had met a man named Jack. She and Jack had accumulated a lot of stuff—houses, clothes and cars. Then Jack ran off with another woman. Although she didn't have Jack, she kept the house, cars and clothes, but she came to understand that she really missed Jack. So the punch line of the song was, "I've got cars, clothes and house, but I ain't got Jack."

There are many people who have houses, cars and clothes, but don't have Christ. Today, many people have lost sight of the fact that houses are not homes and buildings are not churches. Many couples save money to buy a new house and forget, or do not pay any attention to, what it takes to make it a home. Many churches across this country are building fine buildings; paying much attention to the design and structure, but little attention to what it takes to transform a group of people into a

*A church without the presence of God is just a building. Unless the Lord builds the house, it is all in vain.*

church. A home without love is just a house. A church without the presence of God is just a building. Unless the Lord builds the house, it is all in vain. Ultimately, there can be no success in our homes, in our churches, at school, in sports, in education, in politics or in our careers without God. God makes the difference!

In Psalm 127, the psalmist tells us that unless God builds the house our building is in vain. He includes in this the church, city and family. Unless the Lord is in the building of the church, it is all in vain. Unless the Lord is in your work, in your efforts and in your job, it is all in vain. Unless the Lord builds the family, we will ultimately fail. The psalmist says that even a diligent man who works from early morning until late evening cannot hope for success without God's blessing and sanction. The psalmist reminds us that although human effort is important, ultimately we need to place our trust in God.

## Dealing with Opposition

The psalmist draws from the historical experience of Nehemiah. After the Israelites had been in exile and gone back to Jerusalem, they had the task of rebuilding the Temple, the house of God, after it had been destroyed during the invasion of King Nebechadnezzer and the Babylonian army. Nehemiah, Ezra, Haggai and Zechariah were all a part of this rebuilding process.

As soon as they began building the temple, opposition arose against them. Nehemiah 4:21–23 tells us that Nehemiah had them to watch, work and pray. He put some people on the walls with spears while others worked on the building, and he had other people praying. They watched, worked and prayed all day and night, stopping only to wash their clothes.

> One of the things we need to understand is that anything you do for God will meet with opposition from Satan.

One of the things we need to understand is that anything you do for God will meet with opposition from Satan. You can't build one Sunday School classroom without opposition from Satan. In my talking with pastors from Maine to California, there has never been a building program at the church that did not meet with opposition. When somebody tries to do something to build the kingdom of God, the devil, with his deceitful self, will get in the minds of people to form opposition against it.

God gives us good news in the Gospel of Matthew 16:18, where He said, *"Upon this rock I will build my church; and the gates of hell shall not prevail against it."* Isn't that good news? God said that ultimately we have the victory if we build our ministry, our church and our lives on the solid rock of Jesus. Jesus built His church on the great confession that He is the living Christ; not on Peter, but on Peter's confession which is our confession, also.

It is significant to know that Jesus was in Caesarea Philippi, a city at the foothill of a mountain that was named in honor of Caesar when He made this statement. This was a city where people worshiped mythical gods of the Greeks. So in the midst of a ruling government that was in opposition, and competing gods, in other words, in the midst of a "hell" situation, Jesus said, *"Upon this rock I will build my church; and the gates of hell shall not prevail against it."*

## Who Do You Say That I Am?

Our problem is in thinking that the church is a religious insti-tution rather than the body of Christ. We will not know what the church is until we know who Jesus is. That is why Jesus asked the question, "Who do men say that I am?" He even got per-sonal and specific, *"Who do you say that I am?" (Matt. 16:15 NLT)* Jesus is asking us the same question that He put to the disciples, "Who do you say that I am?" Peter said, *"Thou are the Christ, the Son of the living God" (Matt. 16:16).* Jesus said to Peter, *"My Father in heaven has revealed this to you" (Matt. 16:17 NLT).*

*Our problem is in thinking that the church is a religious institution rather than the body of Christ..*

We are the body of Christ and Christ is the head of the body. We can't comprehend the church as the body of Christ if we are secularly and carnally minded. Spiritual truth can only be under-stood with a spiritual mind. Carnal minds cannot discern or understand the spiritual things of life. We must be transformed by the renewing of our minds (Rom. 12:2). Have you been transformed? Is your heart fixed and your mind made up? Does the church look like Jesus to you or do you just see a building and a bunch of people?

I am convinced that if we spiritually understood who we are, then we wouldn't act like fools in the church. In my travels across this country, I have been burdened for some churches I've visited because they have carnal-filled leadership. They are not concerned at all about what the Bible says. They see the church as a religious institution.

God tells us not to be unequally yoked in marriage (2 Cor. 6:14) because we need to marry a person that is also spiritual-minded. If you marry a lady who is carnal-minded, she will not understand spiritual things. If you marry a man who is not spiritual-minded, who thinks secularly that two and two must always equal four, he won't understand that in the spiritual world two and two may not be four. Being unequally yoked leads to conflict in the home because both are not of a spiritual mind. Being equally yoked is necessary for the Lord to build the house.

Our blindness to who Jesus is not only affects the church and our families, it also affects our bodies. We wouldn't treat our bodies the way we do, if we understood that our bodies are the temple of the Holy Ghost. There is no way we would put alcohol or nicotine in our bodies if we understood that our bodies are the temple of the Lord. When we actually realize that we are polluting the temple of the Holy Ghost, we will throw away our cigarettes and remove the Coors from our refrigerators.

## Withstanding the Storms of Life

Unless the Lord builds the house, it will not withstand the storms of life. Be assured that there will be some storms in and through life. In his book *Preaching Through the Storm*, Dr. H. Beecher Hicks, says that all of us are in one of three places. We are either heading into a storm, in a storm, or on our way out of a storm. I remember that we were buying our current property at Greenforest, when I first read that. I thought to myself, "To the best of my knowledge I am not in a storm or coming out of a storm. If he's right, then a storm is on the way." Right then I started boarding up and preparing for the storm. When you know the storm is coming you don't just sit and cross your legs. Anybody who lives on the coast will tell you that when the weatherman says "A storm is coming" they board up the house before the storm arrives.

*Unless the Lord builds the house, it will not withstand the storms of life.*

When you begin a capital campaign, there may not be a storm right then, and you may not be coming out of a storm, but you need to board up. You need to board up with prayer, love, meditation and praise so you will be ready for the storm when it comes. The Bible tells us that there will be opposition. The devil is not happy with expanding any part of the kingdom, so we need to board up. We need to board up with the solid rock of Jesus. Jesus said, "Upon this rock I build my church and the gates of hell, no opposition, shall prevail against it."

## The One Mission of the Church

A church that is built on the solid rock of Christ, will always keep the main thing the main thing. Jesus came to seek and to save. If we are not seeking and saving we are not keeping the main thing the main thing. Jesus had one agenda, one mission. If we are going to be a church that is built on the Solid Rock, then we need to have one mission.

What does a church with one mission look like? It is one where ruins find a remedy; where cursed finds a cure; where hurt finds healing; where broken hearts find love; where burdens find blessings; where victims find victory; where guilty finds grace; where ruthless finds redemption; where doom finds deliverance; and where polluted finds pardon. The church that is built on Christ transcends any human and supersedes any mortal capacity.

What does a church that is not built on the Solid Rock look like? It looks like a motel for people who are just passing through on Sunday, probably on the way to a ball game. It looks like a vacation spot where people come on Easter and Mother's Day, just to get away for a little while. It looks like a zoo where people come to watch how others behave. It looks like a museum where people can only remember what it was like in the good old days. It looks like a fashion show where people come to display the latest fashion and attire. It looks like a picture show where people come to sit and look at the movie. They watch the pastor, watch the choir and don't do anything but sit there. It looks like a ceramics shop where everybody has a chip on his or her shoulder and everybody has to be handled with care. It looks like an icehouse where people are cold and give other people the cold shoulder.

> *The church that is built on Christ transcends any human and supersedes any mortal capacity.*

If we build the church like Jesus says, it will be a lighthouse giving light to a dark and stormy world. It will be a hospital where saints and sinners find healing. It will be a lifeboat throwing out a lifeline to save those who are drowning in sin. It will be a signpost guiding the lost to the saving knowledge of Jesus Christ.

## Summary

We may build great cathedrals and conquer all the failures of the past, but only what we do for Christ will last. God wants us to build the church on the solid rock of Christ. He knows that

> *We may build great cathedrals and conquer all the failures of the past, but only what we do for Christ will last.*

we will be opposed. That's why He wants us to have a solid foundation so we can withstand life's storms. We must stop viewing the church as a religious institution. Through our spiritual minds, we must see the church as the body of Christ and ourselves as the temple of the Holy Spirit. Then, the Lord will build the house so our building will not be in vain.

**Nehemiah 4:1–6**

¹But it came to pass, that when Sanballat heard that we builded the wall, he was wroth, and took great indignation, and mocked the Jews. ²And he spake before his brethren and the army of Samaria, and said, What do these feeble Jews? Will they fortify themselves? Will they sacrifice? Will they make an end in a day? Will they revive the stones out of the heaps of the rubbish, which are burned? ³Now Tobiah the Ammonite was by him, and he said, Even that which they build, if a fox go up, he shall even break down their stone wall. ⁴Hear, O our God; for we are despised: and turn their reproach upon their own head, and give them for a prey in the land of captivity: ⁵And cover not their iniquity, and let not their sin be blotted out from before thee: for they have provoked *thee* to anger before the builders. ⁶So built we the wall; and all the wall was joined together unto the half thereof: for the people had a mind to work.

# A Mind to Work

When Nehemiah returned to Jerusalem, they began a mighty work rebuilding the temple. Although the temple was there—that is, the sanctuary was there, the chandelier was in place, everything was all there, but the walls were not up complete. The walls were torn down and the gates were burning. I always think of those walls as our ministries. Although the chandelier is brightly shining in the sanctuary, the walls of Sunday School, Bible Study and discipleship training are burning down. So our charge is to be about the business of building up the walls. We ought to be about the business of building up the gates so that the fire that is consuming them may go out and we may have strong ministries again.

> *We ought to be about the business of building up the gates so that the fire that is consuming them may go out and we may have strong ministries again.*

When Nehemiah came back to this situation, the temple was built, but the walls were not joined together. They began to join together the walls and put the ministries together. To make it more contemporary, we might say that the Trusteeship would no longer stand by itself in the work of keeping up the facilities and maintaining the cleanliness of the church. The Stewardship Ministry would no longer stand by itself in keeping up with the monies of the church. The Deaconship would no longer stand by itself in ministering to the people and assisting the pastor. Instead they would all be joined together. So the call is for the joining together of the ministries.

As they began to join the walls, opposition rose up again, first from the outside, and then from the inside. Sanballat and Tobias began to mock them saying, "Will the new Israel do anything?" Today, they might mock us saying, "What about this feeble group of Christians who bought this $5.6 million facility? Will they keep it up? Will they clean the chandelier? Will they keep the floors glossy? Will they keep up the walls of the church? Will they keep the bathrooms clean? Will it no longer be a place of respectability and reverence for God? What will they do with their feeble selves? Even if they have a church, their ministries are so pitiful and weak that if a fox walks up to it or a gnat stands on it, it will probably fall. If a mosquito sneezes on it, it would go away. Will the people have a mind to work? That is what is being asked, today.

## We are in Revival

We are in revival. You don't have to have a revival to be in revival. God has given us a mind to work and we appreciate those who have done so much thus far. We can say that God has blessed our

*God is asking us, "What have you done for me lately?"*

church with the grace of work. Somebody said that Greenforest is the "workingest" church she has ever been in. We have a mind to work, but we cannot rest on our laurels. We cannot sit back on yesterday or last year. God is asking us, "What have you done for me lately?" We must answer that question, whether or not we have a mind to work.

Our work has been good thus far, but it is time for us to join our ministries together. There should be no separation between us whatsoever. Everything should be in harmony. It is time for the ushers to join with Christian Education. The Stewardship Ministry and the Trusteeship should be in harmony with the

Deaconship. All should be joined together as one under Christ because there is but one God.

## Easy Church

The call is for us to have a mind to work. However, we are reminded that not everybody has a mind to work. Those who don't, want something easy. They like everything easy. They want to have something easy to cook, like one of those microwave dinners. They have an easyboy chair. They want to live on easy street, have an easy job and make some easy money. They even want an easy church.

It's what I call a "spiritual life of riley syndrome." They want church that doesn't last long—one hour and everybody goes home. They want somebody to affirm God's goodness for them. They want somebody to say amen for them, somebody to say their praise and somebody to say "Thank you, Jesus" for them. They want an easy church where nobody challenges them about their living or their giving. They don't want to hear the Word of God that cuts two ways. They want it to comfort, but never disturb. That's what you call easy church.

Amos, that great prophet of justice and righteousness warned us, *"Woe to them that are at ease in Zion" (Amos 6:1).* We don't need easy church. We don't need easy living because God has challenged us to be like him and have the mind of Christ. Woe unto us if we don't want to be challenged in our living and in the giving of our tithes.

Every time we talk about tithing, somebody wants to talk about raising the budget. We're talking about spiritual renewal when we talk about tithing. There is a relationship with God that is only possible if you are obedient to him in relationship to your money. Jesus knew it when He said, *"For where your treasure is, there will your heart be also" (Matt. 6:21).* If you say your heart is with God and your money is

> There is a relationship with God that is only possible if you are obedient to him in relationship to your money.

somewhere else, watch out! There is inconsistency in your life between what the Word of God speaks and what you are doing. We don't like to hear that because that's not easy.

I propose that we not be too much at ease in Zion. I propose that we not suffer from that dreadful spiritual life of riley syndrome. I suggest that we prepare our minds for the work of

God as the Word of God instructs, teaches and admonishes us to do.

## Leadership Makes a Difference

The first thing the Word tells us relative to having a mind to work is that leadership can make a difference. Those of us, who are in leadership positions, be it on the ministerial staff, Deaconship or Trusteeship, whether we sing in the choir or stand at the door, can make a difference. Leadership makes a difference in the way an usher smiles at people when they come through the door. It makes a difference in how an usher says, "May I take your baby to the nursery?" It makes a difference in how the Stewardship Ministry handles requests for a certain amount of money. It makes a difference in whether or not the deacon's life is a model. Leadership makes a difference. Where there are weak pastors, there are weak churches. Where there are weak deacons, there are weak Deacon Family Ministries.

We're talking about togetherness and one person can make a difference. Nehemiah was only one person, but he made a difference. Joshua was only one person, but he was the one who led them around the walls of Jericho seven times before the trumpet sounded, the shout was made and the walls came tumbling down. Paul was only one person, but he wrote two-thirds of the New Testament. Jesus was only one person and there is a one-man theme in the Bible. Jesus, our savior was one man and He made a difference. Nehemiah had the leaders to call themselves together. Those who were mixing mortar joined with those who were using the trowels. When the leadership joined together, they made a difference.

> *When the leadership joined together, they made a difference.*

## An Idle Mind is the Devil's Workshop

An idle mind is the devil's workshop. You've heard old folks say that before and it is true. If some of you went with the pastor and the deacons to the hospitals sometimes, you wouldn't get bent out of shape over the little things that upset you, e.g., the color of the walls. What difference does the color of the walls make when there is a lost world and people dying? The problem is that an idle mind is the devil's workshop.

A story is told of a church that split. There was an argument and half of the congregation went one way and the other half went the other way. One day, the deacon was showing the new pastor around. When they got to the sanctuary, the deacon pointed to the piano and told the new pastor, "That's what we split about. That piano over there." The pastor said, "What!" The deacon said, "That's what we split about. That's why you're here. It's because of that piano right there." The pastor pondered this and then asked, "Well, what was the problem?" The deacon said, "Some thought the piano should sit on this side and others thought it should sit on that side." The pastor said, "Let me ask you one thing before we go any further. Which side were you on?" The deacon replied, "I don't know, Pastor. I can't remember, but you can bet I was on one of them."

> *Show me a church that is arguing and fighting and I will show you an idle church.*

Show me a church that is arguing and fighting and I will show you an idle church. They're not working. They don't have a mind to work. If you have a mind to work, you cannot be in neutral. It's like a car. You have to be in neutral to idle. An idle mind is the devil's workshop. Jesus tells us that in order to find our lives, we must lose our lives. In order to gain our lives, we must spend our lives. The people must have a mind to work.

## A Godly Mind

A mind to work is a godly mind. Having a mind to work is having a God-approved, God-ordained and God-anointed mind. God tells us in Proverbs 6:6 to look at the ant. Look at how he goes about his work. He doesn't have a ruler over him, yet he works for the harvest and stores it up.

We are reminded in Corinthians and in Philippians 2:5 that Christ had a mind to work. We should have the mind of Christ. *"Let this mind be in you, which was also in Christ Jesus"* (Phil. 2:5). Christ had a mind to work. When He was on the throne with His Father and saw a dying world, He made the journey from the throne to the cradle, to the cross and back to the throne. When He was in His earthly father's house, Joseph's house, He worked as a carpenter. The Bible says, *"And Jesus increased in wisdom and stature, and in favour with God and man" (Luke 2:52).* He must have had the mind to work because when He was 12 years old, He was found in the temple saying, *"Wist ye not that I must be about my Father's business?" (Luke 2:49).* He must have had a mind to work when He prayed, *"Not My will, but Thine, be done" (Luke 22:42).* If we're going to be like Jesus, then we have to have a mind to work.

## Summary

What should our response be to God's call to have a mind to work? Our response should be what Paul tells us in Romans 12:1, *"I beseech you therefore, brethren, by the mercies of God, that ye present your bodies a living sacrifice, holy, acceptable unto God, which is your reasonable service."* I beg you by the mercies of God, to respond to God's call. If God has been good to you, if He has been merciful to you, then present yourself wholly unto Him. Will He accept you? Yes, He will. You have not sunk so low that God will not accept you. Present yourself, as a living sacrifice with a mind to work for it is indeed your reasonable service.

**Exodus 35:4–10 (NIV)**

[4]Moses said to the whole Israelite community, "This is what the LORD has commanded: [5]From what you have, take an offering for the LORD. Everyone who is willing is to bring to the LORD an offering of gold, silver and bronze; [6]blue, purple and scarlet yarn and fine linen; goat hair; [7]ram skins dyed red and hides of sea cows, acacia wood; [8]olive oil for the light; spices for the anointing oil and for the fragrant incense; [9]and onyx stones and other gems to be mounted on the ephod and breastpiece. [10]All who are skilled among you are to come and make everything the LORD has commanded."

**Exodus 36:3—7 (NIV)**

[3]They received from Moses all the offerings the Israelites had brought to carry out the work of constructing the sanctuary. And the people continued to bring freewill offerings morning after morning. [4]So all the skilled craftsmen who were doing all the work on the sanctuary left their work [5]and said to Moses, "The people are bringing more than enough for doing the work the LORD commanded to be done." [6]Then Moses gave an order and they sent this word throughout the camp: "No man or woman is to make anything else as an offering for the sanctuary." And so the people were restrained from bringing more, [7]because what they already had was more than enough to do all the work.

# One Great Day of Giving

Can we imagine a day when the pastor tells the congregation to stop the offering plate because we have given too much? Wouldn't that be a great day of giving? Many pastors are reluctant to preach about money and many believers are afraid to hear any preaching about money. I'm thankful to God that I've never had that problem or concern. You see I have a hard time separating my soul from my substance. I cannot separate God's grace from my gratitude. I'm thankful that God allows me to keep my house, cars and children. I know that the house, cars, children and grandchild that I call mine, are not mine but His. I cannot separate my soul from my substance and God's grace from my gratitude because it all belongs to God.

Now I stand in Moses' shoes, under the anointing of the Holy Spirit, leading God's people in "One Great Day of Giving," just as he did at Mount Sinai. Under the commandment of God, Moses called "all" of God's people together and commanded them to bring a freewill offering to God for the Tent of Meeting, a place where man would meet God, even there in the wilderness of Mount Sinai. We see the unfolding of this narrative as the people immediately left Moses and returned with all kinds of gifts. Some brought fine linen, others brought gold and silver, and others brought precious gems and acacia wood. Those who were wise-hearted offered up their skills to do the work of God. There was a great outpouring of giving. There was such great giving that those who had been assigned to build the Tent of Meeting had to stop working to tell Moses that the people had given too much. They told Moses that the people had given enough. So Moses sent a decree to stop the offering because they had more than enough.

> *There was such great giving that those who had been assigned to build the Tent of Meeting had to stop working to tell Moses that the people had given too much.*

## Two Methods of Giving

In the Bible, there are two methods of giving that are approved by God. The first is regular systematic giving. Paul talked about it in 1 Corinthians 16:2: *"Upon the first day of the week let everyone of you lay by him in store, as God hath prospered him, that there be no gatherings when I come."* In other words, on the first day of the week set aside a regular amount to give to God (that usually encompasses the tithe), give it systematically and on regular intervals.

The second way of giving that is approved in the Bible is not as frequent, but much more dramatic, and that is *"One Great Day of Giving."* Let's look at a few biblical examples. When Solomon prepared to build the temple there was One Great Day of Giving. As Nehemiah, Ezra, Zechariah and Haggai rebuilt the temple, there was a call for One Great Day of Giving. In the New Testament, at the feast of Pentecost, there was a call for One Great Day of Giving.

## The Five Acts of "One Great Day of Giving"

There are five acts in particular I would like for us to reflect upon as we prepare for One Great Day of Giving.

247

1. **There must be *an act of worship* in any One Great Day of Giving.** The text tells us that the Israelites brought an offering from what they had and lifted it up unto the Lord. The Hebrew word for lift is "heave." They lifted it up as an act of worship. A more descriptive translation would be that "they took from their personal pile, and

   *They waved their offering as an act of worship.* brought it to the church and piled it up." They

   brought fine linen, brooches, bracelets, silver, gold, onyx gems and acacia wood, and then lifted it up as a heave offering.

   In verse 22 of the text, we learn that they waved their offering as an act of worship. As gross as it may sound to our twentieth century contemporary minds, I want us to envision the people lifting goat hair and the skin of sea cows, and waving it saying, "Thank you, God. Thanks for bringing us out of Egypt and leading us across the Red Sea. Thanks for forgiving us for making the golden calf. Let us hold up our offering and wave it to our Lord on this great day!"

2. **One Great Day of Giving must be an *act of willingness*.** Throughout the text, emphasis is placed on

willingness. Exodus 35:5 says, *"Whosoever is of a willing heart..."* Verse 21 says, *"Every one whose heart stirred him up, and every one whom his spirit made willing..."* Verse 22 says, *"Both men and women, as many as were willing..."* Our giving must be an act of willingness. If we are not willing, we need not give because God loves a cheerful giver.

I wanted to know if there had ever been a One Great Day of Giving at any church in this country, so I did some research. I found out that the First Baptist Church of Dallas, Texas, raised $1.8 million on One Great Day of Giving. I found out that the the Mount Carmel congregation that formerly worshiped in our church, a congregation about the size of ours, just eight years ago, raised $1 million on One Great Day of Giving for the purchase of the Family Life Center (the gymnasium) we now own.

Then I ran across a little church in Houston, Texas with about 300 members. They accomplished their goal of $480,000 by pledging 100 percent of their income for forty days. How was that possible? They did it by many taking second jobs. They also went to the farmer's market and bought food for soup and bread, and then ate at the church. The executives, doctors and lawyers all ate soup and cornbread at the church. They even serviced each other with their skills. If anybody needed a doctor, lawyer, plumber, electrician or any other type of service, they supplied it through their congregation. They serviced each other while eating soup and cornbread at the

*One Great Day of Giving has to come from our own internal willingness.*

church for forty days. I also learned that this church never lost its fire because what they were doing meant more to them than money. I'm not asking anyone to eat soup and cornbread. I'm asking that you reflect on what God has done for you and what you see Him doing in this church. Our motivation for One Great Day of Giving has to come from our own internal willingness.

3. **One Great Day of Giving must be *an act of privilege.*** It is a privilege for us to be able to give God what is already His. It is also a privilege that God graciously and happily receives what is already His anyway. It's a privilege because God already owns it. It reminds me of what my children do to me when they take my credit card and

buy me a gift. When they bring the gift to me I have to be happy about the gift, but then they turn around and wear it.

**4. One Great Day of Giving must be an *act of inclusion*.**

Everybody was included. Moses spoke to the entire congregation, not just to some. I'm sure there are a few people who would love to give $10–$20,000 if we would put their names in lights and fixed it so they got the glory instead of God, but that's not God's way. Moses did not go on the Jerusalem television to advertise and sell Moses dolls for One Great Day of Giving; neither did he tell every family to sell Moses dolls. He didn't go on the Mount Sinai radio and tell every family to sell tent pins or send in a certain amount of money before his crystal kingdom fell down, so they could be rewarded. He didn't tell the people to send a certain amount of money and he would send them a prayer cloth so their prayers would be answered. As a matter of fact, I don't see any of that anywhere in the Bible. There is no promise of what God will do for us. The Bible doesn't talk about individual

> *It is also a privilege that God graciously and happily receives what is already His anyway.*

blessings for us anywhere. There is only the promise of the joy we will have, which will be more than enough.

The text tells us that those who did not have silver or gold or onyx gems brought acacia wood. I believe the Holy Spirit put this here for our edification. What is acacia wood? It's a hard wood that makes good furniture. Acacia wood is a thorny bush that grows in a barren land and it can't be pulled up without puncturing your hands. Those

*They brought a thorny bush to the Lord and with bleeding hands lifted it up and waved it before Him.*

who had little had to go down by the valley and pull up a thorny bush. They brought a thorny bush to the Lord and with bleeding hands lifted it up and waved it before Him. It is an act of inclusion.

5. **One Great Day of Giving must be an *act of lavishness*.** The people brought so much that it was more than enough. The size of the Tent of Meeting was not lavish or extravagant compared to today's standards, nor was it anywhere near the likes of Solomon's temple. It was to be mobile and taken with the people, and the Ark of the Covenant was to be housed in it. The gifts they brought were lavish and the outpouring was lavish, so much so

that they had more than enough. Moses told the people to stop the offering because they had too much. They gave the way God gives. We often talk about the tithe, but now we're talking about the offering.

## Summary

I'm reminded of the father whose prodigal son returned. Lavishly, the father told his servants to kill a fattened calf for his son. He told them to put a fine ring on his son's finger and robe him. Why? Because the father in this story represents God and our Father is an extravagant God. As Mary bowed at Jesus' feet with the alabaster box

*The people brought so much that it was more than enough.*

and the expensive perfume, some despised and rebuked her; yet, she took the expensive perfume and poured it on Jesus' feet. Jesus told the others to leave her alone for she was only giving as God gives. She was giving in the mode of Christ.

Christ took a little boy's lunch—a couple of fish and five loaves of bread—and there were baskets left over. Christ told the fishermen, cast out into the deep side and throw your net on the right, and the boat began to sink because there was so much. Christ always gives enough and even more. On the day of the wedding at Canaan when the wine ran out, Christ took the water in six pots and turned it into wine that the old skins could not hold. It was more than enough. Christ gave more than enough on Calvary when He gave His unlimited love and grace. When Christ gave His love, He gave enough for each and every sinner. Our call today is to make this One Great Day of Giving a day of an abundant, willing offering from all of us.

**Exodus 13:21–22**

²¹And the LORD went before them by day in a pillar of a cloud, to lead them the way; and by night in a pillar of fire, to give them light; to go by day and night: ²²He took not away the pillar of the cloud by day, nor the pillar of fire by night, *from* before the people.

# Lord, Lead Us Again

## Part 1

During the Easter weekend, many of us find ourselves glued to the T.V. watching a movie produced and directed by Cecil DeMille entitled, *The Ten Commandments*. Although he represented the main characters in this African setting as European, we are still able to learn a biblical lesson of how God leads and guides His people. The movie is an example of how western civilization has brainwashed and misled us; not only relative to secular history, but also biblical history. It is a very powerful movie, yet misleads us to believe that the characters of the Old Testament history, like Moses, the Egyptian Pharaoh and the Midianites, were all white. That's really beside the point. I just thought I would enlighten us with a little biblical Black history.

The main point of the movie was to teach us that God leads and guides His people. We have the assurance that God does lead and guide us. We must seek God's leadership in our capital campaign giving.

## The Israelites Exodus Experience

In the Israelites' Exodus experience, we see that God guided them in the way they should go in order to teach and mature them. It's difficult to know where to begin this exposition, but I wish to begin with Joseph, the patriarch. Joseph went down into Egypt (Africa), found favor with Pharaoh, and was elevated from one position to another after many struggles. After being reunited with his family, because of the favor Joseph had with the Egyptians, his family moved there. Many years later Joseph died.

*We have the assurance that God does lead and guide us.*

After Joseph's death, a new Pharaoh ruled Egypt, one who had never heard of Joseph and his favor with the Egyptians. The Israelites had multiplied so rapidly that Pharaoh feared them, so he enslaved them and had them make bricks out of straw to build the pyramids and other monuments for the Egyptian kingdom.

God raised up a deliverer, Moses. Moses went into the wilderness where he met Jethro the Midianite, who gave him his daughter, Zipporah, to wed. One day God met Moses in a burning bush and commanded him to go back to Egypt and tell Pharaoh to let His people go. Moses did so in obedience to God, but Pharaoh did not listen because his heart was hardened. So God sent Moses back to Egypt and sent one plague after another to soften Pharaoh's heart. Finally, the last plague, which killed all of the Egyptians' firstborn sons, softened Pharaoh's heart and he set God's people free. The Israelites' firstborn did not die because God had them kill an unblemished lamb and place its blood over their doors so when the death angel came, it would pass over them and their sons would live. This was only a foretaste of what the blood of Jesus would do for us later.

During this time of chaos, God's people were instructed to leave Egypt, and so they did. God led them in a great procession in which they carried Joseph's bones. He led them in their journey through the wilderness with a cloud by day and a pillar of fire by night. He led them in a very supernatural, yet natural way. In those days when caravans stretched some 50 miles through the desert, to keep up with one another, the natural process was to have blazing coals in the front wagon. During the day, the people would pour water over the coals so the steam would come up like a cloud and could be seen at the end of the caravan. At night, they didn't have to put water on the coals because of the light of the blazing fire. God supernaturally built on what they already knew. This time they did not have to use coals. None were needed because God provided the clouds and fire supernaturally.

## The Greenforest Exodus Experience

Those of us who have been around the Forest for a while know that Greenforest had its own Exodus experience. Twenty-four years ago, there was a congregation of African Americans and Caucasian Christians. One Sunday morning, most of the Caucasians left the congregation, leaving a handful of African Americans and a few Caucasians totaling about 25 Christians to carry on this church. Then God began to raise up a people and a pastor. God started a marvelous revival and the people began to multiply.

Later, some thirteen years ago, there was a need for a larger sanctuary. God led us and provided us a way to buy this facility when we didn't have the money to buy it according to the bank, but we did. Afterwards, 450 families made the journey to the new church in celebration of what God had done for us. God has been leading and guiding us all along the way. The providential hand of God has been upon us.

## Accessing God's Guidance

How do we know God's lead? Please know that the answer is ignited and accessed through prayer. Our prayer is, "Lord, lead us again." The Lord led us in the move to our present facility. He led us to a bank

*The providential hand of God has been upon us.*

that would make a loan to us based on faith. He led us to a Christian banker who told us that based on secular numbers, there was no way for us to receive the loan, but that he was going to give it to us anyway. The Lord led us to increase our giving to be able to pay our bills when we moved in this facility. He led us to start a credit union and a Christian school so that our children could be educated God's way. Lord, lead us again!

## Forgetfulness

Our problem is one of forgetfulness. We have forgotten how God led us in the past. How quickly the people of God, the Israelites, forgot how he led them out of slavery by one plague

*God leads us from dangers we've never seen and don't even know exist.* after another. How quickly they forgot how He sent the death angel to smite the firstborn of the Egyptians so they could have time to get out of Egypt. Instead of thanking God, they wanted to go back and stomp in the straw pit of slavery rather than dance into the land of promise.

Many of us are that way. How quickly we forget that it was God who led us to achieve what we have in school and in business. It was God who led us through the red seas of life, yet we are so quick to forget. Our capital campaign giving must be based upon God's faithfulness to us in the past. Our future giving should reflect God's past faithfulness.

## Three Ways God Leads Us

There are three ways God leads us. First, **God leads us by His own protection**. This was clearly demonstrated with the Israelites. God did not lead them by the way of the enemy, the

Philistines, even though it was the closest route to the promised land, He knew they were weak and would turn back to slavery. God leads us from dangers we've never seen and don't even know exist. God protects us from things we don't know about. God orders the steps of a good man or woman to protect us.

Secondly, **God leads us by our recollection of past experiences with Him**. The way we know God leads us for future references is to build on the memories of what He's done in our past. The Israelites built on the memory of God's past guidance. They even carried the bones of Joseph out of Egypt. According to history, there were several other coffins carried out of Egypt, but they carried the bones of Joseph because God promised him that he would not be buried in slavery. Joseph represents four generations of God's blessing from the seed of Abraham—Abraham, Isaac, Jacob and Joseph. We, like the Israelites, are the seed of Abraham, but we must build on the recollection of what God has already done and what God has promised.

> *We must build on the recollection of what God has already done and what God has promised.*

Thirdly, **God leads us with supernatural powers**. God led the Israelites with a cloud by day and a pillar of fire by night.

The Bible says that the cloud and the pillar of fire stayed before them. I believe that God still leads by supernatural powers, but He does not waste supernatural power on believers who have little faith. As a matter of fact, God does not lead by supernatural power until our natural power runs out. In other words, God does not step in with supernatural power until we have done all that we can do in the natural.

When I cast the vision to expand the church where I pastor, I wanted to leave room for some supernatural power. I wanted

*God does not lead by supernatural power until our natural power runs out.*

to make the vision big enough that we could see God in a cloud by day and in a pillar of fire by night. We can cast the vision based upon our ability, but we have to make it big enough so that when we've done all that we can do, God can step in and show out.

I did the same with my personal commitment to the campaign. When I made my personal commitment, I made it big enough that I could experience the supernatural power of God. I wanted to make it beyond my means so I could see God in a cloud and a pillar of fire. I wanted to leave room for God to show up and show out.

## God's External and Internal Guidance

God leads us externally and internally. There are seven words that talk about external and internal guidance.

- God leads and guides us externally by **circumstances**. God provides us with circumstances and situations so we will know that it was His hand that led us. I know it was the hand of God that led me to be pastor of Greenforest. One day, some twenty-three years ago, I left home going to my home church in downtown Atlanta, Ebenezer Baptist Church. Instead, I went looking for Greater Travelers Rest, got lost and walked into Greenforest. The rest is history. There have been circumstances in our lives that let us know it was the hand of God that led us.

- God leads and guides us externally by counsel that comes through **testimonies**. So as we hear the testimonies, listen to God's leadership because He could be counseling us.

- God leads and guides us externally by **consequences**. There are consequences of past blessings and giving. Twelve years ago, I made a $25,000 commitment to "Together We Buy" (Our financial plan and theme for purchasing the current Greenforest sanctuary and facility).

I now have to look back over twelve years of blessings and decide, How much more must I give?

- God leads and guides us internally by **common sense**. God will not lead us to make a decision or commitment that He wouldn't help us fulfill.

- God leads and guides us internally by **compulsion** and **consciousness**. God will lay an impulse on our spirit about what to give. It may be in a quiet voice from God when we're lying down to sleep, or when we're driving somewhere, but God is going to place the right amount to give in our spirit. And if we have the wrong amount, God is going to say to us, "Come on give me a break, have I not been good to you?" Yes, we will hear God's voice in our consciousness.

- God leads and guides us by **contentment**. Whatever our decision, we should make sure that we are at peace with God and ourselves. That's contentment. It's good to be at peace with God.

## Summary

I have given you seven "C's." I wish to conclude with three "P's"—pray, peace and push. Pray until you have peace. After you have peace, push forward. Trust the Lord and He will lead us again.

**1 Chronicles 29:1c, 3, 5b, 6, 9**

¹ᶜThe palace *is* not for man, but for the Lᴏʀᴅ God.

³Moreover, because I have set my affection to the house of my God, I have of mine own proper good, of gold and silver, *which* I have given to the house of my God, over and above all that I have prepared for the holy house…

⁵ᵇAnd who *then* is willing to consecrate this service this day unto the Lᴏʀᴅ?

⁶Then the chief of the fathers and princes of the tribes of Israel, and the captains of thousands and of hundreds, with the rulers of the king's work, offered willingly…

⁹Then the people rejoiced, for that they offered willingly, because with perfect heart they offered willingly to the Lᴏʀᴅ: and David the king also rejoiced with great joy.

# A Pure Vision and a Sacrificial Gift

## Lord, Lead Us Again—Part 2

God has provided us with a biblical pattern of giving to the capital campaign. I want to encourage us to follow God's biblical pattern because that's the pattern we should follow. Let's follow God's biblical pattern as we continue to pray, "Lord, lead us again!"

## A Vision Defined

A vision is a projected view of what we are coming to be in the future. A vision is always out there somewhere. If we are there, it is no longer a vision. A vision is always in the future. If it's not in the future, then it's not a vision, but a purpose or mission statement.

## A Sacrifice Defined

A sacrifice is giving up something of value for something of a greater value. To sacrifice we first have to give up something of value. I remember the year baseball player Barry Bonds was chasing Mark McGuire's home run record. I recall his manager, Dusty Baker, asking him to make a sacrificial bunt. Bunting means to hit the ball just enough to get it down on the ground so your teammate can advance to another base. I couldn't believe Dusty Baker was asking this man, who was chasing a home run record that could stand for years and mean millions

*To sacrifice we first have to give up something of value.* of dollars, to sacrifice himself for the team. In obedience to his manager, Bonds laid down a perfect bunt, his teammate advanced to the next base and they went on to win the ball game. Because of his obedience, God blessed him and he not only hit the 70 home runs needed to break the record, but 73.

In 1 Chronicles 29, we see a pattern of sacrificial giving to build a house for the Lord that begins with a perfect vision. The central character is David who is known for being the greatest sinner and the greatest saint of the Old Testament. David was the one who messed up, but got cleaned up. Most of us resemble

him. David had a vision to build a house for the Lord. He realized that because of his age he wouldn't be able to see the house
completed so he chose his son, Solomon, to complete the building of God's temple.

Many of us, including myself, have reached an age where we
realize that we are not building a church for ourselves. We are
building a church for future generations as a witness to God for
worshippers and souls. David said, *"The palace is not for man,
but for the LORD God" (1 Chron. 29:1).* He declared that although
he was old, he was still going to personally give above and
beyond his tithes and offerings out of his love for God and God's
purpose.

## Over and Beyond

Capital campaign giving calls for us to give over and beyond
our tithes. This is a biblical pattern of God. David chose to give
over and beyond his usual giving and gave of his personal
account. David's gift was unusually personal.   *Capital campaign giving*
The Hebrew word for what David gave is *calls for us to give over and*
*beyond our tithes.*
segulla. Segulla is treasure of great importance
to any king. The king actually owns all of the land, but his

271

personal segulla is his security blanket. It's his insurance in case he loses his kingship. It's like the money we set aside for real hard times, like a famine or depression. So David's giving was sacrificial and over and beyond his tithes.

## A Biblical Pattern of Giving

Let's look closer at King David's giving. The text tells us that he stood before the people and asked, *"Who then is willing to to consecrate his service this day unto the LORD?" (1 Chron. 29:5b).* All of the leaders of the Father's house, the leaders of the tribes, the captains of the army and the officers of the kingdom gave.

*A vision without a task or a task without a vision is slavery.* In today's terms it would have been all of the ministerial staff, the deacons, trustees, all of the ministry leaders, musicians, choirs and ushers. All of the assembled gave, and they all gave sacrificially. The congregation then gave and David rejoiced and the leaders rejoiced and blessed the name of the Lord. This is our biblical pattern for giving.

## No Vision, No Task

The problem is that many churches have no vision and no task. The Bible says, *"Where there is no vision the people perish"(Prov. 29:18).* Without a task, the vision will perish. We are blessed when God gives us a vision. However, it is one thing to have a vision and another to have a task along with the vision. A vision without a task or a task without a vision is slavery. A vision without a task is lusting, but a vision with a task is victory. God has shown me that He will provide for a godly vision. This vision is a pure vision because it's to build a house for the Lord, not a house for us, but the Lord's house.

> *The vision must be to build the house for God, not for man.*

Herein lies several spiritual truths relative to a pure vision and a sacrificial gift.

- **Sacrificial giving begins with a pure vision.** The vision must be pure. The vision must be to build the house for God, not for man. I would like to share something God has revealed to me in my twenty-three years of pastoring. God revealed to me that if we cast the vision, He would send people to fulfill it. God said to me, "McCalep, if you cast the vision, write it and make it plain, I will send people your way to fulfill it." That means that everyone sitting in my congregation is part of God's provision to fulfill this vision. God led us where we are today to help fulfill His vision and His vision is pure. Therefore, our sacrificial giving must be pure.

- **Sacrificial giving begets sacrificial giving.** In other words, sacrificial giving produces more sacrificial giving. Our capital campaign consultant told us a true story of a young lady in another campaign who was a single parent raising several children. Although she had learned obedience in tithing, there was nothing else. The young lady prayed and prayed, and God revealed to her that she could give her lunch money that was only $3.00 a day. One Sunday, she gave a testimony that her $3.00 a day would add up to more than $3,000 over a three-year period and that was going to be her gift. The next Sunday, a man who had made a commitment of $40,000 heard of what this single mother was doing and was convicted to increase his sacrificial giving. Sacrificial giving produces more sacrificial giving.

*Sacrificial giving produces more sacrificial giving.*

- **Sacrificial giving is the food that is needed for a living body**. We are faced with the challenge of a capital campaign because we are blessed to be a part of a living church. Anything that's dead needs no nourishment.

A story was told about a church member, a woman, who complained about the church always asking for money. One day when the woman was whining and complaining as usual, another woman stepped forth to share a testimony with her. The woman said, "I need to tell you a story." She didn't tell the woman at the time that it was her own personal story. She said, "There was a couple that had a baby and were excited even before the birth of the baby. They built a nursery on their home that cost them money. Then they spent money for prenatal care. When the baby was born, there was food to buy, formula, milk and diapers. They even set aside money for the high-priced car insurance they would have to buy when the baby became a teenager. Next, it was the burden of paying for a college education, but halfway through the college education, the child was killed in a car accident, and then they had no more money to pay."

*The dollar amount is not important. It's the sacrifice that's important.*

The point of this story is that we are blessed to be a part of a ministry that's alive. If the ministry were dead, we wouldn't have to do any sacrificial giving. A dead ministry wouldn't cost us anything.

- **Sacrificial giving means equal sacrifice, not equal gifts**. Each gift is as important as another. The dollar amount is not important. It's the sacrifice that's important. That's why Jesus told the story of the widow's mite in the Gospel of Mark. He told all of the big shots, who had committed much, that the widow had given more than all of them because she had given out of her need. They gave out of their abundance, but she gave out of her living, out of her lunch money. We need to understand that God does not judge us on the amount, but He does judge us on the sacrifice, which simply means that one person's $50,000 may be greater than another person's $250,000 if it's a greater sacrifice.

## Of Thine Own Have We Given Thee

Sacrificial giving to a pure, God-given vision is a privilege and an honor. Some may ask, "Who are they at the church to ask me for money?" My prayer is that anyone thinking that way will catch the spirit of David in 1 Chronicles 29:14. He said:

*"But who am I and what is my people that we should be able to offer so willingly after this sort? for all things come of thee and of thine own have we given thee."*

We are in a position to give back to God what is already His, just as a child who uses his father's money to buy his father a birthday present. My sons have bought me a whole lot of stuff with my money. They present it to me shouting "Happy birthday, Daddy!" That's the position we're in, to give back to God what belongs to Him already. It's His in the first place. We're just in a position to use His money to build a house for Him.

*Sacrificial giving elevates our level of praise.*

## Give and Get Your Praise On

Sacrificial giving elevates our level of praise. Sacrificial giving brings praise to its highest peak. King David asked, "Who then also is willing to sacrifice?" And I ask the same question today, Who then is willing to give sacrificially? After David asked, the leaders gave, the assembly gave, the whole congregation gave and then praise broke out. The widow, as I would imagine, after giving her two mites, got her praise on. Those who gave much got their praise on and those that gave little got their praise on. David rejoiced and the leaders and the people rejoiced. They said, "Bless the Lord!" Someone may be asking, "Why should we bless the Lord?" We should bless the Lord because He has done great things in our lives.

## Summary

God has given us a pure vision and He's calling each of us to give a sacrificial gift. Let us follow the biblical pattern of King David from the leaders through the congregation. It's not equal gifts, but an equal sacrifice over and beyond our tithes and offerings. Let's give to God what is already His and get our praise on!

**Nehemiah 1:1–7**

[1]The words of Nehemiah the son of Hachaliah. And it came to pass in the month Chisleu, in the twentieth year, as I was in Shushan the palace, [2]That Hanani, one of my brethren, came, he and *certain* men of Judah; and I asked them concerning the Jews that had escaped, which were left of the captivity, and concerning Jerusalem. [3]And they said unto me, That remnant that are left of the captivity there in the province *are* in great affliction and reproach: the wall of Jerusalem also is broken down, and the gates thereof are burned with fire. [4]And it came to pass, when I heard these words, that I sat down and wept, and mourned *certain* days, and fasted, and prayed before the God of heaven, [5]And said, I beseech thee, O LORD God of heaven, the great and terrible God, that keepeth covenant and mercy for them that love him and observe his commandments: [6]Let thine ear now be attentive, and thine eyes open, that thou mayest hear the prayer of thy servant, which I pray before thee now, day and night, for the children of Israel thy servants, and confess the sins of the children of Israel, which we have sinned against thee: both I and my father's house have sinned [7]We have dealt very corruptly against thee, and have not kept the commandments, nor the statutes, nor the judgments, which thou commandedst thy servant Moses.

**Matthew 6:21–24**

[21]For where your treasure is, there will your heart be also. [22]The light of the body is the eye: if therefore thine eye be single, thy whole body shall be full of light. [23]But if thine eye be evil, thy whole body shall be full of darkness. If therefore the light that is in thee be darkness, how great *is* that darkness! [24]No man can serve two masters: for either he will hate the one, and love the other; or else he will hold to the one, and despise the other. Ye cannot serve God and mammon.

# Lord, Revive Us Again

## Lord, Lead Us Again—Part 3

It was approximately thirteen years ago when our church engaged in its first capital campaign that led to the purchase of our current facility. Our theme was "Together We Buy." What I remember most about Together We Buy is that it led us into a spiritual revival. It was awesome. We experienced much more of a true, authentic revival during that campaign than we did during our regularly scheduled summer revival. God used money raising to promote faith raising. We raised money to buy this

*If we let God lead us in our capital campaigns, it will result in a spiritual revival.*

church where we are sitting right now, but more importantly, God raised our faith in the process. We raised money, but we grew spiritually. If we let God lead us in our capital campaigns, it will result in a spiritual revival.

## An Old Testament Example

The Old Testament gives us a great example of a spiritual revival. The central character is Nehemiah. Nehemiah is known as the prophet of revival. He was one of the Israelites from Jerusalem who did not return to Jerusalem after they were set free. The Israelites were marched off into captivity by the Babylonian kingdom where they sat there by the river Kebar for many years as punishment of their sins. After seventy years, God had mercy on them and sent the Persian army to overthrow the Babylonian army and government.

So the Israelites were set free and were able to go back to Jerusalem, but all of them did not return. Nehemiah did not return, rather he landed a good paying job as a cupbearer for the Persian king. A cupbearer is one who tastes the food before the king does to make sure it is not harmful to the king. I'm allergic to seafood and often times when we go places where there are appetizers, my wife serves as my cupbearer. She goes ahead of me and tastes the various foods. If any of the food has seafood, she tells me not to eat it.

The Babylonian and Persian governments were known for their political and social uprisings, i.e., overthrowing kings and governments. So the king needed someone to taste his food to see if it was poison. Now for obvious reasons the cupbearers found great favor with the king. Kings loved their cupbearers, and cupbearers were paid extremely well for their risky jobs.

One day, Nehemiah bumped into a home boy who had come back from Jerusalem. Nehemiah asked him, "How are things back home?" home boy said, "I hate to tell you, but the news is not good. Back in Jerusalem and the providence of Judea, things are not well. Although the church is rebuilt, the people are depressed and suppressed. Not only that, but the walls of the temple are torn down and the gates are on fire." Nehemiah being burdened for the people of God began to pray and fast almost instantly. His prayer to God is our prayer, today. Nehemiah said, "O Lord I pray, please let your ears be attentive to the prayers of your servant. And let your servant prosper this day I pray." This prayer was the beginning of a great spiritual revival that took place after the exile in Jerusalem, under the prayerful leadership of the prophet Nehemiah. I believe we can learn from looking at Nehemiah in relationship to what we ought to be doing for a spiritual revival.

## Burdened for the Need

Nehemiah was burdened for the need. If we are going to have a successful spiritual stewardship campaign, we should be burdened for the need. Nehemiah was so burdened that he cried. When we see teenagers at our True Love Waits Conference sitting in the overflow and hanging on the outside of the church because there is no room for them in the sanctuary where they

*If we are going to have a successful spiritual stewardship campaign, we should be burdened for the need.*

can make a commitment to abstain from sex until a holy marriage, it ought to burden us enough that we sit down and cry. We ought to be burdened to reach more teenagers and youth. If we are really going to be successful then we need to be burdened.

We need to be burdened to reach more worshippers for the Lord. The Lord is looking for worshippers today. The Lord is looking for those who will give Him adoration and who will publicly express love to Him. We need to be burdened for places for people to be reached during Fulfillment Hour (Sunday School). Let me clarify so you don't get the wrong idea. This entire campaign is not about space or a building. It's about reaching people for the Lord. If anyone views the campaign as being for the purpose of building, and not reaching people to fulfill the purposes of God, then you are spiritually blind.

## Fast and Pray

Nehemiah was not only burdened to the point of weeping for the need of God's people, but he also fasted and prayed. Before he began the work of rebuilding the wall and fixing the burning gates, even before he asked the king if he could go down to Jerusalem to help the people, he fasted and prayed. It was later that he asked and found favor with the king, went out, observed, and then started the process of rebuilding the wall and the gate. What we're asking is that we all pray, pray and pray. However, prayer is really incomplete without fasting.

*If anyone views the campaign as being for the purpose of building, and not reaching people to fulfill the purposes of God, then you are spiritually blind.*

Some of you may be wondering when the pressure of manipulation is going to begin. The very nature of the campaign does not allow anyone to be pressured into giving. No one will ever be told what to give at any point in the program. Our financial involvement is a decision between the Lord and us. Giving is a part of worship, but giving must come from the heart to please God, not from our checkbook to satisfy a program. If anyone is feeling we are involved in secular deception, then somehow you have been spiritually blinded.

## Spiritual Cataracts

The problem is that many of us have developed spiritual cataracts from trying to serve two masters. Trying to serve two masters will cause you to have spiritual cataracts. We cannot

*Trying to serve two masters will cause you to have spiritual cataracts.*

serve God and mammon; we will love one and despise the other. Many of us have developed spiritual cataracts over the years. It's not that we're blind, but that we're not seeing as we should because we have gotten caught up in serving the world instead of totally serving God. Look at what Jesus says in Matthew 6:21, *"Where your treasure is there your heart will be also."* In other words, if we put our money in places and things, and creature comforts, then these are the things we love.

Once someone handed me an envelope and said, "Pastor, take my tithe." The person gave me $5.00. I said to myself, "Where do you work? Whoever you work for is paying you illegally. It is against the law to be paid that little of money." Figure it out. This person is being paid far below minimum wage and they need to report their employer to the government to see if it is at all possible for them to receive a rebate. There is no way in the world,

> *We can have money and love God, but we can't love money and love God.*

in this day and time, that $5.00 can be a tithe. It's not a tithe of social security and it's not a tithe of welfare. Even if we are drawing unemployment while we're off from work, it's not a tithe.

Some of you may be wondering how is it that some of us seem to be more willing to sacrifice for the capital campaign. The answer is, *because we love the Lord*. We will serve whom we love. We can't love the world and God at the same time. We can't love money and God at the same time. We can have money and love God. In fact, He wants us to have it. We can have money and love God, but we can't love money and love God. We will serve one and despise the other.

Matthew 6:22 tells us that the light of the body is the eye. The eye is the body's lamp. If the eye is good, everything else is good. If the eye is bad, everything else is bad. If the eye is good, there is light. If the eye is bad, there is darkness. If the eye is good, our thinking will be good. If the eye is bad, our thinking will be bad. We have spiritual cataracts if we see this campaign as a scheme to get our money. We have spiritual cataracts if we see the church as a religious institution and not the body of Christ. We have spiritual cataracts or we are spiritually blind, if we see the preacher as a con artist and not a man of God. We have spiritual cataracts if we see the capital campaign as a money-raising scheme and not a spiritual plan to fulfill God's purposes.

## Summary

The question is, How is our eyesight? Our eyes do go bad. That's why I wear glasses. Two of my sons have had laser oper-

> *We have spiritual cataracts if we see the capital campaign as a money-raising scheme and not a spiritual plan to fulfill God's purposes.*

ations to correct their vision. I'm suggesting that some of our eyes have gone blind and we need the Lord to perform a little laser surgery on us like He did with the blind man at Bethsaida (Mark 8:22–26). The man was not completely blind, he could see a little, but he wasn't seeing right. Jesus led him to the outskirts of town, away from the crowd, so He would be able to really touch him right. Jesus touched the blind man and then asked him, "What do you see?" The blind man said, "I see men, but they look like trees." Jesus said, "You're not seeing right." So Jesus touched him again and said, "What do you see now?" The blind man said, "I see everything and it looks like it ought to look."

Some of us are like the blind man was at first. We have received the first touch from God, the touch of salvation, but we need a second touch. We need to let God perform a little laser surgery on us. Let Him cut away some of that stuff we have developed by trying to serve the world and serve Him at the same time. We need to let God touch us with His strong hand of compassion, conviction, love and mercy. Those of us who see the church as an organization, need Jesus' second touch. He needs to keep touching us until we say, "I see the church and it looks like the body of Christ. I see the preacher and he looks like a man of God. I see the capital campaign and I know it's for a spiritual revival. I see Jesus and He looks like God the Father, God the Son and God the Holy Ghost. I can see everything clearly now!"

**2 Chronicles 29:15–19, 25–31, 35–36 (NLT)**

[15]These men called together their fellow Levites, and they purified themselves. Then they began to purify the Temple of the LORD, just as the king had commanded. They were careful to follow all the LORD's instructions in their work. [16]The priests went into the sanctuary of the Temple of the LORD to cleanse it, and they took out to the Temple courtyard all the defiled things they found. From there the Levites carted it all out to the Kidron Valley. [17]The work began on a day in early spring, and in eight days they had reached the foyer of the LORD's Temple. Then they purified the Temple of the LORD itself, which took another eight days. So the entire task was completed in sixteen days. [18]Then the Levites went to King Hezekiah and gave him this report: "We have purified the Temple of the LORD, the altar of burnt offering with all its utensils, and the table of the Bread of the Presence with all its utensils. [19]We have also recovered all the utensils taken by King Ahaz when he was unfaithful and closed the Temple. They are now in front of the altar of the LORD, purified and ready for use."

[25]King Hezekiah then stationed the Levites at the Temple of the LORD with cymbals, harps, and lyres. He obeyed all the commands that the LORD had given to King David through Gad, the king's seer, and the prophet Nathan. [26]The Levites then took their positions around the Temple with the instruments of David, and the priests took their positions with the trumpets.

*continued on page 292*

**2 Chronicles 29:25–31, 35–36 (NLT) continued**

²⁷Then Hezekiah ordered that the burnt offering be placed on the altar. As the burnt offering was presented, songs of praise to the LORD were begun, accompanied by the trumpets and other instruments of David, king of Israel. ²⁸The entire assembly worshiped the LORD as the singers sang and the trumpets blew, until all the burnt offerings were finished. ²⁹Then the king and everyone with him bowed down in worship. ³⁰King Hezekiah and the officials ordered the Levites to praise the LORD with the psalms of David and Asaph the seer. So they offered joyous praise and bowed down in worship. ³¹Then Hezekiah declared, "The dedication ceremony has come to an end. Now bring your sacrifices and thanksgiving offerings to the Temple of the LORD." So the people brought their sacrifices and thanksgiving offerings, and those whose hearts were willing brought burnt offerings, too.

³⁵There was an abundance of burnt offerings, along with the usual drink offerings, and a great deal of fat from the many peace offerings. So the Temple of the LORD was restored to service. ³⁶And Hezekiah and all the people rejoiced greatly because of what God had done for the people, for everything had been accomplished so quickly.

# From Commitment to Celebration

## Lord, Lead Us Again—Part 4

Spiritual commitment leads to spiritual celebration; therefore, let's prepare to celebrate! Our Old Testament text gives us a marvelous biblical example of how sanctification and commitment lead to rejoicing and celebrating. There are two main characters in this text, King Hezekiah and the Levites. King Hezekiah is a fairly young king who takes over the kingship at age twenty-five. He is known as the king of reformation or revival. God uses King Hezekiah to prepare His people to live godly.

> Spiritual commitment leads to spiritual celebration.

King Hezekiah was a good king, but his father, King Ahaz, was just the opposite. King Ahaz was a very bad king who actually closed up the temple and prohibited worship of the true God during his reign as king. However, one of the first things

293

King Hezekiah did was to open the doors of the church and institute worship again. After taking over the kingship, King Hezekiah cleansed the temple. He called the Levites and priests together and commanded them to cleanse and sanctify the temple, and when everything was finished they made offerings.

They made many sin offerings using bullocks, rams and goats. The animals were brought to the altar for the atonement of the sins of the people so they could be reconciled with God. Afterwards, Hezekiah called the Levites together to begin the celebration. He had the Levites sing some of the Psalms of David and Asaph. We don't know the Psalms he chose, but after the singing of the Psalms, they concluded by bowing before the Lord in worship.

## God Prepares His People

King Hezekiah rejoiced because God had prepared the people, and He did it suddenly. As I considered that, I couldn't help but think of how quickly God prepared us for this capital campaign. It was not that long ago when the vision was first cast, yet in just three quick months we found that God had prepared us very well. We too can rejoice because the Lord has so quickly and suddenly moved in our lives, yet there still rests a problem. The problem is that some of us still have not sanctified ourselves. The problem is one that I call an unclean and unsanctified house.

The Bible tells us that King Hezekiah and the Levites threw out the idol Gods and prepared themselves for the work of the Lord. When Joshua got ready to cross over the river of Jordan, God told him to sanctify himself. Sanctification is a prerequisite for victory. God does not give victory to an unsanctified people. God does not allow unsanctified people to overcome. So how do we sanctify ourselves? If we are going to sanctify ourselves, we have to throw out some old stuff. We sanctify ourselves by throwing out the idol gods, confessing and repenting, fasting and praying, but not necessarily in that order.

> *Sanctification is a prerequisite for victory.*

## Throw Out the Idol Gods

What do we need to throw out to be sanctified? Anytime there is something in our lives that is keeping us from doing the will of God or not giving all of our love to God, then it constitutes an idol god. Whatever is blocking our total affection to the Lord or whatever we are doing that we know is out of God's will, that's our idol god. If gossip, pornography, cigarettes, T.V. or beer is our idol god, then we need to throw them out. We have confessed that our bodies are the temple of the Holy Ghost, and if that be so, then these things should not dwell within us. If sports are our idol gods, then throw them out. Football is an idol god to many men in this country. Shopping is an idol god to many women in this country. If these are our idol gods, then throw them out!

> *Whatever is blocking our total affection to the Lord or whatever we are doing that we know is out of God's will, that's our idol god.*

I find it interesting that even the brass serpent that brought healing to the people just by looking upon it, was thrown out of the temple. God revealed to me that we could so easily worship the wrong thing just as some of the people worshiped the serpent. If we don't watch ourselves, we can find ourselves guilty of worshiping the new sanctuary. A lady confessed to me a while back saying, "I'm glad I joined Greenforest while we were in the old church, because if I had joined later, upon entering this sanctuary, I would have been worshiping the chandelier." We have to be careful as she was careful. We can worship the pastor and even the Bible, but God wants us to worship Him. There are things that are so close to God—like His church building, His pastor and His written Word—that if we aren't very careful, we can worship them instead of God.

## Equal Sacrifice

Our sacrificial commitment should at least equal the sacrificial sin offerings of the people of the Old Testament. The Israelites sacrificed a lot of animals for their sins—rams, bullocks and goats. They brought so much that the priest couldn't prepare it all. The good news is that although our sins are many, we don't have to bring one sin offering to the church. Why? Because Jesus, the perfect sacrifice, is our sin offering. So we don't have to bring any goats, rams or bullocks. We don't have to bring a sin offering for the atonement and the reconciliation of our sins, but we can bring God an offering of praise.

> *There are things that are so close to God—like His church building, His pastor and His written Word—that if we aren't very careful, we can worship them instead of God.*

We can bring God a sacrificial praise offering and an offering of thanksgiving. Romans 12:1 (NIV) says, *"Therefore, I urge you, brothers, in view of God's mercy, to offer your bodies as living sacrifices, holy and pleasing to God—this is your spiritual act of worship."* We don't have to bring a sin offering, but I believe anytime we are asked to make a sacrificial commitment to God, our sacrifice ought to at least equal the sacrifice of those who had to give sin offerings. I don't know the equivalent of six hundred rams to our praise and thanks offering today, but it's not equal numbers or equal gifts, it's equal sacrifice that matters to God.

## Orchestrated Praise

When God so quickly prepares a congregation for commitment and sanctification, we ought to orchestrate praise. It has not been a long time since God started preparing us for this day; therefore, we ought to orchestrate praise. After the Levites had consecrated themselves, Hezekiah said, "Now it's time to celebrate."

> *Anytime we are asked to make a sacrificial commitment to God, our sacrifice ought to at least equal the sacrifice of those who had to give sin offerings.*

Hezekiah said, "Let me orchestrate some praise." I know some folks, particularly church folks, who don't think praise should be orchestrated, but right here in the Bible, Hezekiah orchestrated praise. He called the Levites and he told them to pump up some praise. In today's terms, he said, "Pump it up!" He set forth the dancers, the harps, the trumpets, the psalteries, the drums, the flute, the string instruments, the cymbals and the high cymbals. Then he said to the Levites, "Now sing a song for me, but I want one of David's songs." Then Hezekiah said, "Let the praise begin!"

There is a word called *shabach* that means "to shout." There is another word called *halal* and it means "hilarious, crazy praise." Halal comes from the word hallelujah. If we really want a breakthrough, then we should give the Lord a crazy praise, something that doesn't make sense. When Jonah needed a breakthrough, he gave God some crazy praise. When Joshua needed a breakthrough, he gave God some crazy praise.

> *When God so quickly prepares a congregation for commitment and sanctification, we ought to orchestrate praise.*

## Summary

God is so faithful. We don't have to wait until the church is built to praise Him. We can shout in advance. We can get our praise on now! If you have been praying for some stuff to happen in your life, you don't have to wait to give God a victory. You can give Him a victory right now! Give God some crazy praise right now!

# Part Four:


# The McCalep Group

# The McCalep Group

The McCalep Group are stewardship consultants who are committed to "doing stewardship God's way." Led by its founder, George O. McCalep, Jr., Ph.D., the McCalep Group specializes in helping churches bring their stewardship ministry into compliance with scripture. Our mission is to transform believers into a life of obedience relative to giving. The McCalep stewardship approach is based on the belief that:

- All ministries, including stewardship, should comply with God's Word.
- Stewardship is about faith raising, not money raising.
- Teaching biblical stewardship principles will create a spiritual awakening throughout the church and a surprising discovery of dormant gifts and talents in the congregation.

- Believers will experience the joy of giving when they give according to scripture.
- Any church can enjoy a successful stewardship ministry through the faithful carrying out of a deliberate, systematic program that is based on scripture.

## Our Services

We help build and grow churches. The McCalep Group provides expert guidance in developing church-wide tithing programs, capital campaigns and 501C3 community development corporations. Our products include:

- **God's Progressive Giving Plan**: The McCalep approach to tithing and giving that churches can implement themselves following the guidelines in Dr. McCalep's book, *Faith Raising vs. Money Raising*, and/or with the help of Dr. McCalep's stewardship seminars and workshops.
- **The McCalep Capital Stewardship Model**: The McCalep approach to capital fundraising for ministry expansion and the acquisition of land and buildings. An onsite consultant guides churches through the implementation of this program.
- **Management of Acquisition, Expansion and Building Projects:** Through our partnership with the Green Forest

Church Development and Management Consultant Corporation, we offer a turnkey solution to all your acquisition, expansion and building needs. Our services include, but are not limited to:

- Application for 501C3 status

- Development of a 501C3 financial management infrastructure

- Development of master plans and architectural layouts

- Loan assistance and financial packaging

- Training and assistance in construction supervision

- Project planning and management

- **Program Development**: The creation and implementation of custom-designed programs to meet any need. Through our partnership with the Green Forest Church Development and Management Consultant Corporation, we will:
  - Assess needs

  - Define goals

  - Develop a project plan

  - Manage the project's implementation

  - Train people to manage the program

  - Provide ongoing support on a consultative basis

## The Advantage of Choosing The McCalep Group

The McCalep Group is a biblical, faith-based ministry that offers a competitive edge in the African American church community. We believe this is true because of the integrity, reputation, experience, and success record of the ownership. Dr. George O. McCalep is the owner and lead consultant. His qualifications include:

- He is an African American minister who is currently pastoring. He is fully aware of the operation, personalities, and profile of the African American church.

- He has a proven record in the area of church stewardship, including spearheading capital campaigns.

- He has demonstrated leadership skills in a history of lifetime successes that encompass athletics, academics, business and his current pastorate.

- He has a proven record of respectable, good relationships with pastors throughout the African American Community and is known as a pastor's pastor because of his longstanding efforts to help pastors in the area of church growth. Pastoral knowledge and support are an essential key to the success of any stewardship campaign.

- He has a heart for churches and a passion for kingdom building.

## The Consulting Team

Our consulting team is highly qualified and anxious to serve.

Our team members are:

- Christians.
- Culturally sensitive.
- Selected and trained by the owner and, likewise, having his spirit and experience.
- Filled a Christ-like spirit.
- Expecting a spiritual awakening and faith raising to occur from our efforts.
- Spiritually gifted for the task of implementing a capital campaign.
- Proficient in project management and recognize the need for hands-on guidance as well as continuous follow-up.

# Epilogue:

# Discovering the Joy of Giving

# Discovering the
# Joy of Giving

The joy of giving is the ultimate stewardship experience. It is giving from the desire to please God and build His kingdom. *The Holman Bible Dictionary* defines joy as the "happy state that results from knowing and serving God." There is joy in knowing that what you give is advancing God's kingdom. Your life's focus becomes fulfilling God's purposes; not just for you individually, but more importantly, for His kingdom here on earth. Thus, giving becomes your lifestyle and you actively seek opportunities to give of your time, talents, money and influence.

True joy comes from a right relationship with God. Jesus tells us in John 15:4, *"Abide in me, and I in you. As the branch cannot bear fruit of itself, except it abide in the vine; no more can ye, except ye abide in me."* Jesus wants us to abide in Him so that our giving will bear great fruit. In John 15:11, He goes on to say, *"These things I have spoken unto you, that my joy might remain in you and that your joy might be full."* God takes joy in our obedience and He rewards us with a joy that is full and complete when we serve Him.

I pray that the following messages will help bring you to this next level of stewardship, the level that I believe is the ultimate stewardship experience—the joy of giving.

**Leviticus 27:30**

And all the tithe of the land, *whether* of the seed of the land, *or* of the fruit of the tree, is the LORD'S: it is holy unto the LORD.

**Malachi 3:8 (NIV)**

Will a man rob God? Yet you rob me. But you ask, "How do we rob you?" In tithes and offerings.

**2 Corinthians 8:7 (NIV)**

But just as you excel in everything—in faith, in speech, in knowledge, in complete earnestness and in your love for us—see that you also excel in this grace of giving.

# Discovering the
# Joy of Giving

### Part 1

Training wheels are used to help people, especially children, learn to ride a bicycle. I can recall, as a young boy, when I learned to ride a bike without support or help from anyone, not even training wheels. It happened on the dirt road in front of my family's home. I would ride and I would fall, then get back up and ride and fall and get back up again and again. I don't know how many times I fell, but I kept trying until I finally got it. In one day, I not only learned to ride my bike, but I also learned to stand up and ride it with one or no hands. I was having fun on that dirt road when I got a big idea. I wanted to see how close I could come to Dr. Chambers' car before cutting around it. So I rode right towards his car. Then at the last minute when I cut away, my bike slid from under me and went under the car. What was a glad day became a really sad day. My brand new bike was totaled on the same day that I received it. I should have had training wheels.

If we want to discover the joy of giving, then tithing provides our training wheels. We live under grace; therefore, giving for the New Testament covenant church is not about legalistic tithing according to the Mosaic Law. Although tithing represents one of many laws given to the Israelites, and although we don't live under the law, tithing is still a good way to discover the joy of giving. It is where biblical giving begins.

> *If we want to discover the joy of giving, then tithing provides our training wheels.*

## Grace Giving

Studies show that only about one-fourth of all Christians claim to tithe. When we look at what we really earn across this country, only about one-tenth of all Christians actually tithe. The number one reason many Christians give for not tithing is that they believe they are not under the law, but under grace, which makes it okay to give what they want to give. I don't have a problem with those who say we are New Covenant or New Testament children of God who are no longer under the tithe.

What I do have a problem with is using that as an excuse to give less.

Every New Testament example of giving goes above and beyond the tithe. Absolutely none falls below the tithe. Does God expect His grace-giving children to give less or more? Jesus always raised the bar. He never lowered the bar. In Matthew 5:27–28, He said:

> *"Ye have heard that it was said by them of old time, Thou shalt not commit adultery: But I say unto you, That whosoever looketh on a woman to lust after her hath committed adultery with her already in his heart."*

Jesus tells us that if a man looks at a woman who wore a too tight, too short skirt to work in lust, it is a sin. Did Jesus lower the bar? Is the standard less? Not one time did Jesus expect us to do less than what the law required. We should be glad for grace, but not use it against God.

*Every New Testament example of giving goes above and beyond the tithe.*

## Robbing God

When we don't use our training wheels to discover the joy of giving, we are not stealing from God; we are robbing Him. The question was asked in Malachi 3:8 (NIV), "Will a man rob God?" — not steal from God. When we steal, we take something when no one is looking; but when we rob, we take it in the person's face. When we refuse to tithe, we are saying, "In your face, God! Stick'em up! I know you're looking. I have this weapon called grace that you gave me and I'm going to use it to hold you up. Now, give me everything you have."

In Leviticus 27:30, we learn that the tithe is holy unto God, meaning our tithe is sacred and has been set aside for service to God. The question is, What's holy to us? Golf, tennis, football and shopping are some of the things that are holy to some of us. We don't want to give up those things that are holy to us. So we rob God by giving Him what's leftover after we have done what is holy to us.

*When we steal, we take something when no one is looking;, but when we rob, we take it in the person's face.*

Another way we rob God is with bad math. I've discovered that either we need math lessons or we have a bad misconception of the tithe. A man came to me once and said, "Reverend,

I want to give you my tithe. Please pay my tithe for me." He handed me $5.00. I wondered, "Where in the world does he work?" Let's assume that he rounded his minimum wage to $5.00 per hour and worked the standard 8 hours a day. Eight times five is 40. Now, let's assume he worked five days a week like most people. Forty times five is 200 and 10 percent of $200 is $20, not $5. When we don't take the time to accurately calculate our tithe, we are robbing God.

Not only do we rob Him of the tithe, but we rob Him of the offering too. In other words, we tell God, "I want what's in your front and your back pocket." In Malachi 3:8, not only was the question asked, "Will a man rob God?" but also, How do we rob him? The answer is not only in tithes, but also in offerings. This

*Giving less than what God expects in a freewill offering is also robbing Him.*

whole matter of robbing God with offerings raises a very interesting point because grace givers rob God by claiming that they are living under grace and not under mandatory legal law. So they think it's okay to give a freewill offering, but giving less than what God expects in a freewill offering is also robbing Him. God expects a voluntary freewill offering, and when we fall short of His expectation, we rob Him

## Keep the Training Wheels on

Unlike riding a bike, once we have discovered the joy of giving, God wants us to keep our training wheels. Speaking to the religious Pharisees in Matthew 23:23, God says:

*"For ye pay tithe of mint and anise and cummin, and have omitted the weightier matters of the law, judgment, mercy, and faith: these ought ye to have done, and not to leave the other undone."*

> Unlike riding a bike, once we have discovered the joy of giving, God wants us to keep our training wheels.

In other words, yes we ought to tithe, but without neglecting the higher concerns of Christian living. Jesus said that we should not ignore the important concerns like showing justice and mercy. We are to keep the training wheels on and increase in spiritual matters such as faith, mercy, love, hope and joy.

## Summary

Without question, Jesus endorsed tithing in the New Testament. When we discover the joy of giving, we need to keep our training wheels. The tithe is how we start, but once we get started, we shouldn't stop there. We should go beyond the tithe into the marvelous the joy of giving.

**Matthew 6:19–21**

[19]Lay not up for yourselves treasures upon earth, where moth and rust doth corrupt, and where thieves break through and steal: [20]But lay up for yourselves treasures in heaven, where neither moth nor rust doth corrupt, and where thieves do not break through nor steal: [21]For where your treasure is, there will your heart be also.

**Matthew 13:44 (NIV)**

The kingdom of heaven is like treasure hidden in a field. When a man found it, he hid it again, and then in his joy went and sold all that he had and bought that field.

# Discovering the Joy of Giving

## Part 2

A steward is one who manages another's assets, but carries no sense of entitlement or ownership to the assets he manages. The steward's purpose is to manage the assets for the owner's benefit. It's the steward's job to find out what the owner wants done with his assets and then carry out the owner's purpose. We are stewards of God's creation and His church. It's our job to find out what God wants done with His church, creation and assets, and then carry out God's purposes.

> A steward is one who manages another's assets, but carries no sense of entitlement or ownership to the assets he manages.

Once we understand that we are giving *God's money* to do *God's work*, then we will discover a joy that we have never had when we thought we were giving our money.

## The Parable of the Hidden Treasure

In Matthew 13:44, Jesus tells us that the kingdom of heaven is like a man, walking in a field, who discovers a buried treasure and hides it again. For his joy, he sells everything he has to buy

*It will cost us everything we own to have everything that really matters in life.*

the field where the treasure is buried. This parable has divine significance because it captures the essence of discovering the joy of giving. The man buries the treasure in the field and sells all he has to buy the field. Notice the words "in his joy" in this parable. If you miss these words, you will miss the meaning of the whole parable. For it was in his joy that the man sold all he had and bought the field. There are three spiritual truths to be lifted from this parable:

1. We must be willing to give up everything on earth in order to have everything in heaven.

2. There is a fundamental connection between our spiritual lives and how we handle money.

3. We are most like Jesus when we are giving.

## Giving Up Everything

Although the man knew he had found treasure, he also knew that he couldn't have it because it belonged to someone else. It was on somebody else's property. If we find $10 million in our backyard, we are entitled to it, but if we find $10 million in someone else's backyard, the money belongs to him because it's on his property. Conclusively, it will cost us everything we own to have everything that really matters in life. Like the man in the parable who "in his joy" sold everything he owned to buy the field, so should we, as we discover the joy of giving.

## The Connection Between Our Spiritual Lives and Money

Joy comes when we learn that our hearts follow our possessions. Jesus tells us in Matthew 6:21 that where our treasure is, there our hearts will be also. What is the application and implication of this for us?

> *Joy comes when we learn that our hearts follow our possessions.*

If our hearts follow our treasured possessions, then we should be careful about what we possess. I had an opportunity to view Ford's new Blackwood, double-cab Navigator truck. It's a pretty truck inside and outside, and I would like to have one. I can afford to buy it, but I'm not going to, at least not yet. I can't and won't get it because I'm afraid that my heart will follow it. I know if I had it, I would not want my grandchild to spill anything in it. That tells me that I like that truck too much. I'm not going to buy it because I want to keep my heart for Jesus.

We must be careful that our hearts don't follow our material possessions. Better yet, we must be "ready" to own stuff. Some of us were not "ready" to own homes and that's why our hearts followed them, instead of Jesus. Some of us were not ready to own the cars we drive and that's why our hearts follow them,

*If we love Jesus more, we will give more.* instead of Jesus. Some of us have money in the bank that God wants to use in His kingdom, but we are holding on to it because our hearts are in the bank with the money and not with God as they should be. We need to have a heart for God.

## We are Most Like Jesus When We Give

The Greek word for "Christian giving" is translated "God's grace." If we love Jesus more, we will give more. When we give more, we become more like Him. Christ gave a whole lot. He gave us His joy that our joy might be full. He gave us His life so that we might live. Christians should want their hearts to be like His heart.

## Summary

I've been a tither for a long time, but I'm discovering the joy of giving everyday, and it is such a joy. It is indeed like a man who found treasure in a field, and for the joy of it hid the treasure in the field again, then bought the whole field. For the joy of giving is in knowing Christ, being like Him and seeing Him.

**Luke 3:2–14**

[2]Annas and Caiaphas being the high priests, the word of God came unto John the son of Zacharias in the wilderness. [3]And he came into all the country about Jordan, preaching the baptism of repentance for the remission of sins; [4]As it is written in the book of the words of Isaiah the prophet, saying, The voice of one crying in the wilderness, Prepare ye the way of the LORD, make his paths straight. [5]Every valley shall be filled, and every mountain and hill shall be brought low; and the crooked shall be made straight, and the rough ways *shall be* made smooth; [6]And all flesh shall see the salvation of God. [7]Then said he to the multitude that came forth to be baptized of him, O generation of vipers, who hath warned you to flee from the wrath to come? [8]Bring forth therefore fruits worthy of repentance, and begin not to say within yourselves, We have Abraham to our father: for I say unto you, That God is able of these stones to raise up children unto Abraham. [9]And now also the axe is laid unto the root of the trees: every tree therefore which bringeth not froth good fruit is hewn down, and cast into the fire. [10]And the people asked him, saying, What shall we do then? [11]He answereth and saith unto them, He that hath two coats, let him impart to him that hath none; and he that hath meat, let him do likewise. [12]Then came also publicans to be baptized, and said unto him, Master, what shall we do? [13]And he said unto them, Exact no more than that which is appointed you. [14]And the soldiers likewise demanded of him, saying, And what shall we do? And he said unto them, Do violence to no man, neither accuse *any* falsely; and be content with your wages.

# Discovering the Joy of Giving

### Part 3

According to God's word, we cannot separate our faith from our finances. We may try to separate them, but there is a connection that makes them inseparable. The Gospel of Saint Luke, Chapter 3, is known as the fruit of repentance chapter. I have read this text many times, but it was only recently that God revealed to me that there is a connection between money and the fruit of repentance. Repentance is necessary for salvation and deliverance. Both Jesus and John the Baptist, preached repentance for the remission of sin. There can be no conversion or transformation in us unless we repent, that is, be truly sorrowful about our present spiritual condition and make a complete turn around away from that condition. **Unless we repent, we cannot be changed.**

> *We cannot separate our faith from our finances.*

## What Is the Fruit of Repentance?

What is the fruit or evidence of repentance? How do we know that we have been changed? The answer to each of these questions is when some fruit shows up in our lives. In this text, John the Baptist told the people to clear the way because the salvation of the Lord was coming. He also warned those generations of vipers, the Pharisees, to flee from the wrath of God, which was soon to come. He urged them to repent and be baptized, and not to rely on their relationship to Abraham for salvation, but on the soon coming Messiah, Jesus Christ. The same is true today. We cannot rely our mom or dad's salvation, our growing up in the church or singing in the choir to save us. We must bear fruit, for every tree that does not bear fruit will be cut down.

## How Can We Bear Fruit of Repentance?

In Luke 3:10–14, John tells us how to bear fruit. The verses reveal without question that there is a relationship between our faith and our finances, and that our faith and our finances are inseparable. In verse 10, the people asked the question, "What shall we do?" In verse 11, John tells them to share clothes and food with those who have less. In verse 13, he tells them not to take advantage of people in money matters. In verse 14, he tells them not to extort money or threaten and intimidate people with it.

In the text, the people didn't ask John the Baptist about money or possessions, but about spiritual transformation, yet every answer John gave them related to money and possessions. The people asked him about the fruit of repentance and about how they could bear some fruit. All three of John's answers related to money and possessions. *Many of us do not realize* According to Acts 2:45, the converts eagerly *that earth is not our home.* sold all of their possessions and gave to the needy. This was evidence of their Christianity. Many church members today are missing out on a powerful, joyful relationship with God because they have not connected their faith to their finances.

## Putting Your Money Where Your Home Is

There are many problems that might explain why we relate to money as we do. Some of us are filled with greed, pride and selfishness. All of these things could be the problem, but God has revealed another major problem. Many of us do not realize that earth is not our home. We live under the illusion that earth is our home and we want to have our money wherever our home is. According to Hebrew 11:13, we are strangers, pilgrims passing through earth. We will never discover the real joy of giving until we cast out the illusion that earth is not our home and accept the fact that we are just sojourning through this earth, just passing through.

## Cheerfulness Follows Giving

We so often hear that God loves a cheerful giver; and according to 2 Corinthians 9:7, this is true. However, we need to understand that cheerfulness follows the act of giving. Oftentimes, those of us in the pastorate try to make a drama out of cheerfulness when it comes to giving. We say, "It's giving time. Yeah!"

*When we don't give, we rob ourselves of the source of the joy that God wants us to discover.*

but that's false cheer because the joy follows the giving. It does not precede it. **When we give, joy will follow.** God loves a cheerful giver, but the joy comes after the act of giving. Some of us try to stir up some joy before we give, but it doesn't work that way. We give, and then we become happy.

## Robbing Ourselves of Joy

When we don't give, we rob ourselves of the source of the joy that God wants us to discover. Sometimes when a person discovers the joy of giving, somebody tries to talk them out of it. I've had it happen to me before. I've had people ask me, "How can you give all that money to the church? Do you know what that will buy?" One time, we prayed along side a wife until her husband came down the aisle with tears in his eyes. Immediately

*Another example of robbing someone of the joy of giving is when we pay volunteers.*

after his conversion, he wanted to know what to do. He found out that tithing is a Christian principle for the saved so he began tithing, not only his money, but also his time. Quite confusingly, his wife who asked us to pray with her for her husband's salvation became angry. She accused her husband of spending too much time and money at the church so she left the church. Don't ever rob a person of the joy of giving.

Another example of robbing someone of the joy of giving is when we pay volunteers. A person can be joyfully volunteering and then someone else gets the idea that he or she should be paid. So we agree to pay the person who has been cheerfully doing a good job. Now all of a sudden, he or she starts getting to work late and eventually quits the job. We need to stop trying to pay those who have a joy for volunteering so that we don't end up robbing them of their joy just because we can't understand it. We do it because we say to ourselves, "If I was doing all that, I would want to get paid."

Recently, I tried several times to tip a man for handling my luggage because I realized that he had done more than the

> *If we want a strong prayer life and want to know how to get a prayer through, we need to discover the joy of giving.*

average person would do. I kept trying to tip him until I realized that I was about to rob the man of something greater than the little $5 or $10 I had in my pocket. So I said to him, "Thank you, Brother" and a smile came over his face. He was filled with joy, and to think, I almost robbed him of it. We need to stop robbing ourselves and others of the source of the joy God wants us to discover.

## Giving Empowers Prayer

Proverbs 21:13 (NIV) says, *"If a man shuts his ears to the cry of the poor, he too will cry out and not be answered."* Giving empowers prayer. Isaiah 58:6–10 tells us that God's willingness to answer our prayer is directly affected by whether we are caring for the hungry, needy and oppressed. If we want a strong prayer life and want to know how to get a prayer through, we need to discover the joy of giving.

## Summary

Discovering the joy of giving jumpstarts God's blessings. It opens our fist so we can receive what God has to give us. Some of us are standing with our arms opened wide, but our hands closed in a fist asking God to bless us. God can't give us anything because we don't have open hands to receive it. In order for God to bless us, we have to repent and open our hands by giving. Then, the joy of giving will follow.

*In order for God to bless us, we have to repent and open our hands by giving. Then, the joy of giving will follow.*

## Luke 19:1–9

[1]And *Jesus* entered and passed through Jericho. [2]And, behold, *there was* a man named Zacchaeus, which was the chief among the publicans, and he was rich. [3]And he sought to see Jesus who he was; and could not for the press, because he was little of stature. [4]And he ran before, and climbed up into a sycamore tree to see him: for he was to pass that *way.* [5]And when Jesus came to the place, he looked up, and saw him, and said unto him, Zacchaeus, make haste, and come down; for today I must abide at thy house. [6]And he made haste, and came down, and received him joyfully. [7]And when they saw *it,* they all murmured, saying, That he was gone to be guest with a man that is a sinner. [8]And Zacchaeus stood, and said unto the LORD; Behold, LORD, the half of my goods I give to the poor; and if I have taken any thing from any man by false accusation, I restore *him* fourfold. [9]And Jesus said unto him, This day is salvation come to this house forsomuch as he also is a son of Abraham.

## Luke 12:16–21

[16]And he spake a parable unto them, saying, The ground of a certain rich man brought forth plentifully: [17]And he thought within himself, saying, What shall I do, because I have no room where to bestow my fruits? [18]And he said, This will I do: I will pull down my barns, and build greater; and there will I bestow all my fruits and my goods. [19]And I will say to my soul, Soul, thou hast much goods laid up for many years; take thine ease, eat, drink, *and* be merry. [20]But God said unto him, *Thou* fool, this night thy soul shall be required of thee: then whose shall those things be, which thou hast provided? [21]So *is* he that layeth up treasure for himself, and is not rich toward God.

**Matthew 19:16–24**

[16]And, behold, one came and said unto him, Good Master, what good thing shall I do, that I may have eternal life? [17]And he said unto him, Why callest thou me good? *there* is none good but one, that is, God: but if thou wilt enter into life, keep the commandments. [18]He saith unto him, Which? Jesus said, Thou shalt do no murder, Thou shalt not commit adultery, Thou shalt not steal, Thou shalt not bear false witness, [19]Honour thy father and *thy* mother: and, Thou shalt love thy neighbour as thyself. [20]The young man saith unto him, All these things have I kept from my youth up: what lack I yet? [21]Jesus said unto him, If thou wilt be perfect, go *and* sell that thou hast, and give to the poor, and thou shalt have treasure in heaven: and come *and* follow me. [22]But when the young man heard that saying, he went away sorrowful: for he had great possessions. [23]Then said Jesus unto his disciples, Verily I say unto you, That a rich man shall hardly enter into the kingdom of heaven. [24]And again I say unto you, It is easier for a camel to go through the eye of a needle, than for a rich man to enter into the kingdom of God.

# Discovering the
# Joy of Giving

### Part 4

The Bible gives us three gospel lessons about three rich men. One of these rich men was Zacchaeus, short in stature, as well as, a dishonest tax collector. The Bible refers to another of these three rich men

> *Our behavior is the best evidence of what we really believe.*

as "a certain rich man" and the third as "a rich young man." The conclusive message of all three parables is that obedient stewardship provides evidence of the assurance of eternal life. Please do not misunderstand this statement; obedient stewardship will not save us. We are saved by grace through faith. However, God's Word tells us that obedient stewardship provides evidence of the assurance of eternal life.

Our behavior is the best evidence of what we really believe. First John 5:13 says, *"These things have I written unto you that believe on the name of the Son of God; that ye may know that ye have eternal life, and that ye may believe on the name of the Son of God."* The question may be raised, "What things are written?" The entire Bible was written so that we may know the truth. We all want eternal life; therefore, I'm proposing that according to the Word of God, obedient stewardship provides evidence of the assurance of eternal life, and our behavior is the best evidence of what we really believe; therefore, we should give like we really believe.

## Zacchaeus, the Seeker

Zacchaeus was a rich tax collector, as well as a seeker, who heard Jesus was passing by. Because he was short in stature, he climbed a sycamore tree so he could see Jesus as he passed by. Jesus saw Zacchaeus and confronted him by saying to him *"Zacchaeus! Quick! Come down! For I must be a guest in your home today!" (Luke 19:5 NLT)*. Despite popular opinion that Jesus should not go to Zacchaeus' house, He went anyway. Jesus saved Zacchaeus despite his dishonesty as a tax collector because He loved him. After Zacchaeus was saved, he said to Jesus in verse 8 (NIV), *"Look Lord! Here and now I give half of my possessions to the poor, and if I have cheated anybody out of anything, I will pay back four times the amount."* Jesus replied in verse 9 (NIV), *"Today salvation has come to this house."* Zacchaeus' radical new approach to money proved to Jesus that he had been truly saved. Just the opposite is true in the next two gospel lessons.

## A Certain Rich Man

In Luke 12:16–21, we learn that "a certain rich man's" business had been good. His fruit was so plentiful that he pondered what to do with it all. He decided that the solution was to tear down his old barns and build bigger ones. We too are like the certain rich man. We may not have barns today, but many of us do

> *Zacchaeus' radical new approach to money proved to Jesus that he had been truly saved.*

have portfolios. Some of us have portfolios with Merrill Lynch, but now feel the need to start another one with Edward Jones. We want bigger portfolios for more security. Jesus called the certain rich man a fool. Jesus went on to tell him that his life would be taken that night because he was not rich towards God. The rich man's problem was not that he was rich, but that he was not rich towards God. Jesus knew this because the man was concerned only with himself. Yes, God wants us rich, but rich towards Him first.

## A Young Rich Man

There was a third rich man, "a young rich man." According to Matthew 19:16–24, he approached Jesus and asked what could he do to inherit eternal life. Jesus told him that he had to keep the Ten Commandments and even recited them to him. The young rich man responded with excitement that he had kept the Ten Commandments since he was very young. Jesus then told him that if he really wanted to inherit eternal life, then he should sell all that he had and give it to the poor. This time the young rich man did not respond, but walked away because he had great possessions. Then Jesus said:

> *"A rich man shall hardly enter into the kingdom of heaven. And again I say to you, it is easier for a camel to go through the eye of a needle, than for a rich man to enter into kingdom of God" (Matt. 19:23–24).*

Jesus didn't say that we couldn't enter into the kingdom of heaven if we have money, but that it's harder for those of us who have it.

In all honesty, all of us want money. Jesus didn't condemn money, but said that it was harder for the man who has lots of it. As a matter of fact, it's easier for a camel to go through the eye of a needle than for a rich man to get into heaven. How is this possible? In Jerusalem there is a gate called "The Needle's Eye." I had an opportunity to see The Needle's Eye in the old city of David. It's impossible for a camel to go through The Needle's Eye gate unless he gets rid of all his baggage and gets down on his knees. I hope we see the picture Jesus is painting. He's telling us that we have too many possessions that we need to shed. We need to take off the stuff that makes us arrogant—our degrees, cars and houses—and get down on our knees so we can go through.

*We cannot discover the joy of giving because possessions often own us and it costs us to change our priorities.*

## Stuff and Money

We cannot discover the joy of giving because possessions often own us and it costs us to change our priorities. We have become slaves to our money and our possessions. I know a man who put a beautiful media room in his nice home. The media room is equipped with CDs, DVDs, stereo surround sound, a widescreen television and comfortable theater seating. It even has a special way of popping popcorn. He has all this in his home, but now he can't get to church because he's too busy sitting in his media room.

I know more than a few people who own timeshare property that really owns them. There is nothing wrong with having a vacation spot or taking a vacation, but when someone owns a timeshare, it means they have to use it or lose it. I know a person who had a timeshare vacation scheduled during the time of revival at his church. He shared with me how miserable he was on his vacation because revival was going on at his church and that's where his heart really was, but instead he was sitting out on a beach somewhere miserable. We cannot let our possessions own us.

## Affluenza

As I examined the text, I came to understand that the problem is that we have a disease, the flu of fluency. I call it "affluenza."

There was a television program some years ago called *Affluenza*. It addressed the modern day plague of materialism. Some of the show's findings were that the average American shops six hours a week while spending only forty minutes playing with their children. Recent statistics show that more Americans have declared bankruptcy than graduated from college. Another statistic states that money is a prominent factor in 90 percent of divorces. Why are these statistics as they are? There is stuff that's causing problems in our lives.

I recently visited an area of Louisiana where gambling is permitted. Their statistics showing the relationship of gambling to the number of foreclosures and divorces are horrible. We think going to a casino is not a bad thing, but it's breaking up families. The interesting thing about the television program, *Affluenza*, was that they didn't deal with statistics from a moral issue, but from a pragmatic one. From the world's pragmatic point of view, we are sick and from God's point of view, we are morally sick. It's an evil sickness of affluenza that plagues our both Christians and non-Christians.

**Affluenza is a disease and giving is its cure.** When we discover the joy of giving we realize that God's money has a greater purpose than our affluence. Giving breaks the fever of affluenza because the joy of surrendering to a greater purpose, person and agenda is in giving. Giving breaks affluenza's fever because it enthrones God and dethrones man.

## A Second Chance

Alfred Nobel, after whom the famous Nobel peace prize is named, had a rare opportunity for a second chance at life. He had the privilege of reading his own obituary because when his

*Giving breaks affluenza's fever because it enthrones God and dethrones man.*

brother died, the writer of the paper thought he had died instead. The writer, not intending to be cruel said, "A merchant of death is dead." Alfred Nobel made his money by discovering dynamite. His obituary spoke of him as the man who discovered dynamite that had allowed people to blow up other people using bombs that he discovered and got rich off. Alfred Nobel's obituary gave him a second chance at making things right, and he took advantage of it by donating millions of dollars to people who exemplified humanity and peace.

Most of us will not have an opportunity to read our own obituary, but I would like to challenge us to think about our obituary and write down how we believe it would read. I would also like to challenge us to answer this question: One minute after we die, what will we wish we had given away? Death represents a lost opportunity to give. What can we give now so that when we die, we can have the joy of knowing that we gave all we could to build God's kingdom?

One caution as you think about your legacy...I know most of us want to leave something for our children. I want us to know that in leaving something for our children, we might bless them, but we might also curse them. We need to pray about what we leave our children because if our children don't' have hearts that are rich for God, we will not be blessing them; we will be cursing them.

> *One minute after we die, what will we wish we had given away?*

## Summary

God wants us to prosper, first in spiritual things, and then in worldly goods. The material things He blesses us with are not solely for our personal enjoyment, but to advance His kingdom. The joy of giving comes in releasing ownership of all our "stuff" to the giver of the stuff. Doing so frees us to experience the true

joy of giving without the burdens of life. Our joy is in our sur-
render.

**Ecclesiastes 2:10–11 (NIV)**

[10] I denied myself nothing my eyes desired; I refused my heart no pleasure. My heart took delight in all my work, and this was the reward for all my labor. [11]Yet when I surveyed all that my hands had done and what I had toiled to achieve, everything was meaningless, a chasing after the wind; nothing was gained under the sun.

**Ecclesiastes 5:10–15 (NIV)**

[10]Whoever loves money never has money enough; whoever loves wealth is never satisfied with his income. This too is meaningless. [11]As goods increase, so do those who consume them. And what benefit are they to the owner except to feast his eyes on them? [12]The sleep of a laborer is sweet, whether he eats little or much, but the abundance of a rich man permits him no sleep. [13]I have seen a grievous evil under the sun: wealth hoarded to the harm of its owner, [14]or wealth lost through some misfortune, so that when he has a son there is nothing left for him. [15]Naked a man comes from his mother's womb, and as he comes, so he departs. He takes nothing from his labor that he can carry in his hand.

*continued on page 350*

**Ecclesiastes 5:19–20 (NIV) continued**

¹⁹Moreover, when God gives any man wealth and possessions and enables him to enjoy them, to accept his lot and be happy in his work — this is a gift of God. ²⁰He seldom reflects on the days of his life, because God keeps him occupied with gladness of heart.

**Revelation 3:18 (NIV)**

I counsel you to buy from me gold refined in the fire, so you can become rich; and white clothes to wear, so you can cover your shameful nakedness; and salve to put on your eyes, so you can see.

# Discovering the Joy of Giving

## Part 5

Have you ever done anything that you knew was foolish? If given a choice between money and wisdom, would you choose wisdom over money? If you had a choice between joy and possessions, which would you choose? I would like to challenge us to make the choice between joy and foolishness. I propose that unless we discover the joy of giving, wealth is foolishness.

> Unless we discover the joy of giving, wealth is foolishness.

## The Wisdom of Solomon

Solomon, one of the richest men who ever lived, wrote the book of Ecclesiastes. God used Solomon's wealth to teach us a lesson for today. In Ecclesiastes 5:10, Solomon said, *"Whoever loves money never has money enough."* In other words,

**the more we have, the more we want.** He also said in verse 10, *"Whoever loves wealth is never satisfied with his income."* In other words, the more we have, the less we are satisfied.

In verse 11, he said, *"As goods increase, so do those who consume them. And what benefit are they to the owner except to feast his eyes on them."* In other words, the more we have, the more we realize that it does us no good.

In verse 12 he said, *"The sleep of the laborer is sweet, whether he eats little or much, but the abundance of a rich man permits him no sleep."* In other words, **the more we have, the more we have to worry about.**

In verse 13 he said, *"I have seen a grievous evil under the sun: wealth hoarded to the harm of its owner."* In other words, the more we have, the more we can hurt ourselves by holding on to it.

In verse 14 he said, *"Wealth lost through some misfortune."* In other words, the more we have, the more we have to lose.

Finally, in verse 15 he said, *"Naked a man comes from his mother's womb, and as he comes, so he departs. He takes nothing from his labor that he can carry in his hand."* In other words,

**the more we have, the more we will leave behind.** It's foolish!

## Chasing the Wind

In Ecclesiastes 2:11, Solomon referred to all he had as meaningless, a "chasing of the wind." What does Solomon mean by "chasing of the wind"? Chasing the wind is like a dog trying to chase his tail. It's like trying to sit in a corner of a circular room. It's like trying to put a square peg in a round hole. It's like trying to out run your shadow. Chasing the wind is like trying to accumulate wealth without knowing the joy of giving. It's foolish!

> *Most of us live under the illusion that something we don't have and probably cannot afford will satisfy us.*

Most of us live under the illusion that something we don't have and probably cannot afford will satisfy us. We generally run out of money before we run out of things we think will satisfy us. Solomon never ran out of money. He was so rich that he ran out of stuff to buy before he ran out of money. Solomon said that he refused his heart no pleasure (Ecc. 2:10). He didn't deny himself anything. He had everything, yet he concluded that wealth without the joy of giving is foolishness.

## Prosperity and the Joy of Giving

If we worry about money, that's a good indication that we have not discovered the joy of giving. If we worry about money, that's a good sign that we are not trusting God with our money. If we can trust God for eternal life, then we ought to be able to trust him with our money.

When we discover the joy of giving, we can be prosperous and happy. God never said that we had to be financially poor to be happy. Jesus said in Matthew 5:3, *"Blessed are the poor in spirit."* He meant happy are those who are humble; not broke, as many have misinterpreted. He never meant that we had to be broke financially to be happy, but broken from pride. He grants us the gift of wealth so we can be blessed and bless others. In Ecclesiastes 5:19, Solomon tells us that God can grant us the gift of being wealthy and wise or prosperous and happy, but without the joy of giving, prosperity is foolishness.

*If we can trust God for eternal life, then we ought to be able to trust him with our money.*

## Too Busy to Complain

When we discover the joy of giving, we will be too busy to complain. If we know someone who complains all the time, then that's a good sign that he or she has not discovered the joy of giving. In Ecclesiastes 5:20 Solomon said, *"He seldom reflects on the days of his life, because God keeps him occupied with gladness of heart."* When we sit back and look at what we have and what we don't have, Satan will give us reasons to complain. When we spend time looking at what we want instead of what God wants from us and for us, Satan will give us reasons to complain. This is why in Philippians 4:8 we are told, *"If there be any virtue, and if there be any praise, think on these things."* When we discover the joy of giving, we accept

> If we know someone who complains all the time, then that's a good sign that he or she has not discovered the joy of giving.

our lot in life and become happy in the work God has given us. We won't be able to complain because God will occupy us with joy.

## Summary

In Revelation 3:18, God counsels us to buy gold that has been refined in fire instead of worldly possessions. He is speaking of divine righteousness, which cannot be purchased with money, but comes through faith in our Lord, Jesus Christ. Our faith is refined by fire when we are tested and challenged to choose wisdom over money and joy over possessions. God also tells us to buy a salve for our eyes, a special anointing of the Holy

*Our faith is refined by fire when we are tested and challenged to choose wisdom over money and joy over possessions.*

Spirit, that when placed on our eyes will open them up so we can see Him. When we choose to stop chasing the wind and be happy with what God has given us, and then start using our blessings to bless others, that's when we will discover the joy of giving.

**Acts 20:32–38**

<sup>32</sup>And now, brethren, I commend you to God, and to the word of his grace, which is able to build you up, and to give you an inheritance among all them which are sanctified. <sup>33</sup>I have coveted no man's silver, or gold, or apparel. <sup>34</sup>Yea, ye yourselves know, that these hands have ministered unto my necessities, and to them that were with me. <sup>35</sup>I have showed you all things, how that so labouring ye ought to support the weak, and to remember the words of the Lord Jesus, how he said, It is more blessed to give than to receive. <sup>36</sup>And when he had thus spoken, he kneeled down, and prayed with them all. <sup>37</sup>And they all wept sore, and fell on Paul's neck, and kissed him, <sup>38</sup>Sorrowing most of all for the words which he spake, that they should see his face no more. And they accompanied him unto the ship.

# Discovering the Joy of Giving

## Part 6:
## From Bah Humbug to Merry Christmas

One thing I always look forward to during the holiday season is watching Charles Dickens' television classic, *A Christmas Carol*. I am particularly interested in the main characters Ebenezer Scrooge and Tiny Tim. I watch this classic every year because watching Tiny Tim gives me a good cry. God has delivered me from many things in my life, but the greatest release in my life is when He set me free to cry. Surprisingly, a strange thing happened the last time I watched it. This time it was not Tiny Tim who brought tears to my eyes, but Ebenezer Scrooge. I cried unstoppable tears as I watched his transformed life. The Spirit of Christmas Past, Present and Future had visited him and transformed his life. Once I noticed Ebenezer's new life, I realized that it was his transformed life that made this a classic all these years.

Ebenezer Scrooge was miserable in himself, tight, stingy, grumpy, greedy and always complaining repetitively saying, "Bah humbug!" Bah humbug meant that he had an "I don't care" attitude or as our young people often say today, a "whatever" attitude. Everything about Christmas was bah humbug to Ebenezer until the Spirit of Christmas showed him his past,

*When Christians discover the joy of giving, we discover the real Spirit of Christmas.*

present and future in a dream. This experience transformed him into a bundle of joy. His whole demeanor changed as he ran, leaped, clicked his heels and danced through the streets of London greeting everybody, not with a "Bah humbug!" but with a "Merry Christmas!"

The thing I noticed most about Ebenezer was that he gave. He had discovered the spirit of Christmas in the joy of giving. When Christians discover the joy of giving, we discover the real Spirit of Christmas, The Holy Spirit. Only then will we be able to go from "Bah humbug!" to "Merry Christmas!"

## The Spirit of Christmas Past

If we look at the Spirit of Christmas Past, like Ebenezer Scrooge, we too will possibly see some of the reasons why we act and think the way we do. The Spirit of Christmas Past took Ebenezer Scrooge back to his childhood and showed him that he had never experienced a family Christmas. His father made him stay and study at a private school while everybody else went home for Christmas. All of us are victims and/or products of our past experiences. I can personally remember the hurt of not getting anything for

*All of us are victims and/or products of our past experiences.*

Christmas. Although your circumstances may have been different than mine, all believers have been victims at some point in their lives. We were all victimized when we were in the world one way or another, if it was only thinking the world was our only way of life. Now, the Holy Spirit has moved on our hearts to let go of our victimizing past so that we can receive our present and future life with our Lord and Savior, Jesus Christ. Therefore, we are no longer victims, but products.

## The Spirit of Christmas Present

As we look at the Spirit of Christmas Present, we all should be able to say that this present life of salvation God has granted us just gets "gooder and gooder." As old folks can say, "God are

---
*As we observe the Spirit of Christmas Present, God gets "gooder and gooder."*

---

good." I know this is not correct English, but it best describes the goodness of God. God the Father, God the Son and God the Holy Spirit are some "good God." That's not good English, but it is good theology. As we observe the Spirit of Christmas Present, God gets "gooder and gooder."

## The Spirit of Christmas Future

When we visit with the Spirit of Christmas Future, we find ourselves experiencing either eternal life or eternal damnation. Some of us need a quick trip to hell, but we know that there is no such thing, there's no turning back once a person gets there. Unfortunately some of us will find ourselves like the rich man in the gospel of Luke who wanted to send someone to warn his five brothers to stop drinking all that liquor and acting like fools (Luke 16:19–31). The worst thing about church folks being in hell will be their knowing that they didn't have to be there.

When we visit with the Spirit of Christmas Future, we will be transformed from bah humbug to joy because we will truly realize the joy of eternal life.

## The Spirit of Giving

In this text, Paul reminds the church at Ephesus of the spirit of giving during his farewell, concluding with, *"It is more blessed to give than to receive" (Acts 20:35).* He tells them in modern day terms, "I have tried to lead you by example, and I have not desired anything that is yours for myself that God did not have for me. I have not taken advantage of your generosity. In fact, I have worked for my necessities."

I wonder today if we spiritually understand that it is more blessed to give than to receive? How many of us are more concerned about what we get for Christmas than what we give? There was a time in my life when I was more concerned about what I would get for Christmas than I would give to others, but when the true Holy Spirit of Christmas visited me, Jesus truly became the reason for the season. Like Ebenezer Scrooge, some of us need a visit from the

*When we visit with the Spirit of Christmas Future, we will be transformed from bah humbug to joy because we will truly realize the joy of eternal life.*

Holy Spirit of Christmas Past, Present and Future to move us from "Bah humbug!" to a truly joyous "Merry Christmas!"

## Let the Record Show

I ask the question again, How many of us really realize that it is more blessed to give than to receive? I ask this question again because as Christians our record doesn't show that we believe

*We have a satanic confidentiality cloud over us because we don't want anybody to know what we are giving.*

it is more blessed to give than to receive. So I asked God, "Lord, why does our record not show that we believe it is more blessed to give than to receive?" God revealed to me that at least one of the problems is that we do not have a bold, sacrificial money testimony on giving. A sacrificial money testimony is having a testimony that tells how much money we are sacrificing without bragging. Paul wanted his life to be a testimony, an example. God recently affirmed in my spirit that when it comes to giving in the church, we have been hushed. We have a satanic confidentiality cloud over us because we don't want anybody to know what we are giving.

This leads to another question, Where does a young Christian learn how to give? Where does a young Christian go to see the life of a believer who has been delivered from materialism and bondage? Where does a young believer go to see a Christian who has discovered the joy of giving? I'm not advocating competitive giving, but there ought to be a way someone who has not discovered the joy of giving can hear an authentic, sacrificial money testimony of someone who has. We have praise teams and song leaders to lead us in praise and worship, a prayer team and prayer warriors to lead us in prayer, soul winners to lead us in evangelism and witnessing, but we have no giving warrior testimonies to teach us the joy of giving.

*We have no giving warrior testimonies to teach us the joy of giving.*

Hebrews 10:24 says, *"And let us consider one another to provoke unto love and good works."* I believe the good works in the scripture includes giving. God wants us to give a testimony relative to our giving. Matthew 6:1 warns us not to give to be seen by or to receive glory from men. Instead, we should give according to Matthew 5:16, so that our light will shine before men and praise our father in heaven. We must have a right motive to give a testimony. Our hearts have to be right. We can't hide it under a bushel or be hushed about it.

## Summary

Since we can't beat God's giving, then why don't we join Him? Giving boldly is the greatest testimony of God's lordship in our lives. If we really believe it is more blessed to give than to receive, then why not join the greatest giver in giving? Without question, God is the greatest giver. He gave the greatest gift and that's the reason for the Christmas season. The greatest gift ever given to

*Since we can't beat God's giving, then why don't we join Him?*

us was God Himself, born of a virgin and gift wrapped in swaddling clothes. The wise men brought him gifts of frankincense, myrrh and gold. The New Testament tells us to give a gift of ourselves, to present our bodies a living sacrifice, holy and acceptable unto Him, which is our reasonable service (Romans 12:1). When we are obedient givers, we will discover the joy of giving. That joy will result in thanksgiving. Our thanks will result in praise, and our praise will lead to worship. When we truly worship God with our entire lives, then we will discover the joy of giving.

# Study Guide and
# Teaching Aid

# Study Guide
# Instructions

The following section contains lessons for individual and group study. The lessons are designed to reinforce the principles that were presented throughout this book. Included are:

## Study and Review

Each lesson consists of several study and review questions. These questions facilitate examination of the principles as well as oneself. An answer sheet is provided for these questions.

Attempt to answer the questions on your own first, and then compare your answers to those on the answer sheet.

## Application

The application questions will help you apply these biblical stewardship principles to your personal life and your church. My hope is that through these questions, God will lead you to put what you have learned into practice.

# Lesson One:
# What the Bible Says About Giving

## Objective

The objective of this lesson is for the participant(s) to internalize and apply the five biblical principles of giving:

- The tithe
- Firstfruit giving
- Purposeful giving
- Willful giving
- Sacrificial giving

## Study and Review

1. What is a steward?

2. What does our giving have to do with our relationship with God?

3. Is the tithe (one-tenth) the only acceptable offering to God? Why?

4. What does firstfruit-giving mean? What is considered first-fruit?

5. How do we know if God is really first in our lives?

6. How do we give purposefully?

7. What does 2 Corinthians 9:7 mean when it says, *"Every man according as he purposeth in his heart, so let him give"*?

8. We all know that God loves a cheerful giver. How do we demonstrate willful giving?

9. What happens when we do not give willingly?

10. Why must we give sacrificially? Is it wrong to give out of our abundance?

11. Why did Jesus immortalize the poor widow in Mark 12:41–44?

12. What makes a good steward?

## Application

1. Examine yourself against the biblical principles of giving. Is there any area where you fall short? If so, what will you specifically do to correct it so you can be in a right relationship with God?

2. We only need to be saved once, but we can be delivered many times from many things. From what do you need to be delivered so that you can give biblically?

3. Tithing is not a money issue. It is a faith issue. Is your faith at the level of the tithe? If not, what will you specifically do to grow to the tithe? If you are already tithing, what will you specifically do to grow beyond the tithe?

4. What talents and spiritual gifts has God given you? What are you doing with them? Is there something that God has called you to do that you are not doing?

5. The Bible says that we will reap what we sow. God promises to multiply the seed we sow. What are you sowing that God can multiply?

# Lesson One:
# What the Bible Says About Giving
# Study and Review Answer Sheet

1. What is a steward?

   A steward is someone who manages or takes care of something that does not belong to him. Christian stewards manage all of the resources—money, talents, gifts, possessions—that God has entrusted to them.

2. What does our giving have to do with our relationship with God?

   Our giving acknowledges our acceptance of God as creator and our role as stewards. Our giving reflects our love for God and our gratitude for all He has done in our lives. Stewardship is a matter of putting our faith into action by demonstrating our dependence on God. It is an outgrowth of our discipleship.

3. Is the tithe (one-tenth) the only acceptable offering to God? Why?

   No. God will bless any effort you make when it is done according to His principles. Less than 10 percent is not the tithe, but God will bless your effort if you give the firstfruit willingly, sacrificially and purposefully. Likewise, 10 percent is not the maximum you can give. God is pleased when we give offerings beyond our tithe according to the same biblical principles.

4. What does firstfruit-giving mean? What is considered first-fruit?

Firstfruits are the first and best of whatever we have. Firstfruit-giving means paying God first, before we pay anyone else, including ourselves. It also means giving him our very best.

5. How do we know if God is really first in our lives?

Our checkbooks will tell us if God is first in our lives. When you get paid, is the first check you write to your church?

6. How do we give purposefully?

Purposeful giving is planned giving. It means that we plan in our hearts and our budgets to give to God. We do not wait until the offering tray is passed. When we give purposefully, we accurately calculate our tithe and know how much we are going to give before we get to church.

7. What does 2 Corinthians 9:7 mean when it says, *"Every man according as he purposeth in his heart, so let him give"*?

When you purpose in your heart to give, you commit your-self to a giving plan. It means planning what you give and when. It also means planning to grow in your giving. Commit yourself to giving goals and make them known to those who hold you accountable.

8. We all know that God loves a cheerful giver. How do we demonstrate willful giving?

   Willful giving is reflected in our attitude when we give because we want to, not because we have to.

9. What happens when we do not give willingly?

   God does not accept gifts that are given grudgingly. If we give grudgingly, we might as well keep it in our pockets because God will not honor our giving.

10. Why must we give sacrificially? Is it wrong to give out of our abundance?

    God does not require equal gifts, but He expects equal sacrifice. When we give sacrificially, we honor God because we give of that which is important to us. When we give only from our abundance, we don't miss it and God is not glorified.

11. Why did Jesus immortalize the poor widow in Mark 12:41—44?

    The widow gave out of her living. She gave all that she had. In so doing, she acknowledged God as the source of all of her needs and her complete dependence on Him. The widow demonstrated a sincere and deep love for God which is an example for us today.

# Lesson Two:
# God's Progressive Giving Plan

## Objective

The objective of this lesson is to ensure participants know the components of God's Progressive Giving Plan and the elements that are critical to its success.

## Study and Review

1. Which ministry of the church is responsible for implementing God's Progressive Giving Plan?

2. Describe the recommended organizational structure.

3. What is the role and responsibility of the Budget and Accounting Division?

4. What is the role and responsibility of the Education and Promotion Division?

5. What is the role and responsibility of the Counting Division?

6. What is the difference between budget making and budget raising?


7. What is a unified budget?


9. What is the difference between a unified budget and an auxiliary budget?


10. What five factors undergird the budget-making process? Explain the importance of each.


11. What are the major components of the budget-raising phase?


12. Why is God's Progressive Giving Plan considered a prototype?


14. What are the four promotional Sundays during Stewardship Emphasis Month? Describe what happens on each Sunday.


15. Why is anointed preaching important to the success of God's Progressive Giving Plan?

16. Why should the commitments be written?

17. What is meant by equal sacrifice, not equal gifts?

18. How can testimonies help in raising the budget?

19. Why is it necessary to track the church's past performance?

## Application

1. Is your church receptive to implementing God's Progressive Giving Plan? If not, what obstacles would have to be overcome? If so, what steps would have to be followed to implement the plan?

2. How can you support God's Progressive Giving Plan in your church?

# Lesson Two:
# God's Progressive Giving Plan
# Study and Review Answer Sheet

1. Which ministry of the church is responsible for implementing God's Progressive Giving Plan?

   The Stewardship Ministry

2. Describe the recommended organizational structure.

   The Stewardship Ministry is directed by a chairperson and should include the church's treasurer or business manager, a financial secretary and at least seven to ten other people. The ministry is comprised of three divisions:

   • Budget and Accounting
   • Education and Promotion
   • Counting

3. What is the role and responsibility of the Budget and Accounting Division?

   The Budget and Accounting Division is responsible for the budget-making process.

4. What is the role and responsibility of the Education and Promotion Division?

   The Education and Promotion Division is responsible for the budget-raising process. They are also responsible for educating the congregation and promoting stewardship throughout the year.

5. What is the role and responsibility of the Counting Division?

The Counting Division counts the weekly collections and prepares the bank deposits.

6. What is the difference between budget making and budget raising?

Budget making is the administrative and accounting aspects of planning, organizing and producing the church's annual unified budget. Budget raising is the process of raising the money to fulfill the budget.

7. What is a unified budget?

A unified budget places all money under one budget. It includes all auxiliary budgets and the church's operating expenses.

9. What is the difference between a unified budget and an auxiliary budget?

The unified budget includes all auxiliaries/ministries and the church's operating expenses. An auxiliary budget is for a specific ministry or auxiliary.

10. What five factors undergird the budget-making process? Explain the importance of each.

(1) *A ministry-driven budget* reflects God's will for the church's ministry and is based on faith.

(2) *A unified budget* is a budget where all monies are managed under one budget. The auxiliary ministries do no have separate bank accounts.

(3) *Inclusion* involves many people in the budgeting process. The process is not limited to an exclusive group of people, but instead involves all of the ministry leaders and the congregation.

(4) *Full disclosure* means informing the congregation of all information related to the budget. Every member should be informed of every penny taken in and every penny that is spent.

(5) *Leadership empowerment* gives authority and power to the ministry leaders to carry out the work that has been budgeted. Empowerment eliminates confusion and conflict, and encourages harmony. Leadership empowerment promotes harmony which increases giving.

11. What are the major components of the budget-raising phase?

    (1) Promotional campaign
    (2) Stewardship preaching and teaching revival
    (3) Sunday School and Bible Study lessons
    (4) Written commitments of percentage
    (5) Testimonies
    (6) Performance data
    (7) Financial planning workshops

12. Why is God's Progressive Giving Plan considered a prototype?

God's Progressive Giving Plan is a prototype because it is a proven model that can be duplicated in any church.

14. What are the four promotional Sundays during Stewardship Emphasis Month? Describe what happens on each Sunday.

- *Acknowledgement Sunday:* Members acknowledge God as creator and owner of all things and their roles as stewards.
- *Prove the Tithe Sunday:* Members are asked to test (prove) God's promise by giving a tithe.
- *Commitment Sunday:* The congregation turns in their written commitments.
- *Victory Sunday:* The campaign results are celebrated and God is given the glory.

15. Why is anointed preaching important to the success of God's Progressive Giving Plan?

Preaching is the most persuasive tool for transformation. Preaching that includes teaching of biblical principles of stewardship must be used in the budget-raising phase in order to raise the congregation's faith.

16. Why should the commitments be written?

Our God is a covenant God. A written commitment represents a covenant with God.

17. What is meant by equal sacrifice, not equal gifts?

God asks us to give 10 percent regardless of our level of income. Asking everyone to give the same amount would be unfair. However, percentage giving adheres to the principles of firstfruit, purposeful, willing and sacrificial giving.

18. How can testimonies help in raising the budget?

    Testimonies encourage others to give and help break materialistic strongholds. They teach others sacrificial giving and show how God rewards obedience.

19. Why is it necessary to track the church's past performance?

    Performance data is used for promotional purposes in future campaigns and to lend credibility to the stewardship process.

# Lesson Three:
# Capital Stewardship

## Objective

The objective of this lesson is to define capital stewardship and identify the elements that are key to its success.

## Study and Review

1. What are the two methods of giving that are approved in the Bible?

2. What is the difference between capital funds and the unified budget?

3. Why should contributions to the capital campaign be over and above regular tithes and offerings?

4. How long does a capital campaign usually take?

5. Why is it beneficial to use an outside consultant?

6. How does a church go about selecting the right consultant?

7. What costs should be considered when planning a capital campaign?

8. What is the role of preaching in a capital campaign?

9. What are some spiritual truths that should undergird any capital campaign?

10. What are some of the common obstacles a church must overcome when implementing a capital campaign?

## Application

1. What vision has God given your church to expand His kingdom?

2. Does the vision require a capital campaign? If so, what will it take for your congregation to embark on such a journey?

3. How could a capital campaign bring spiritual renewal in your church?

# Lesson Three:
# Capital Stewardship
# Study and Review Answer Sheet

1. What are the two methods of giving that are approved in the Bible?

   The Bible approves regular systematic giving (usually the tithe) and One Great Day of Giving.

2. What is the difference between capital funds and the unified budget?

   Capital funds are used for expansion or acquisition projects, e.g., building a new sanctuary or purchasing land. The unified budget is for the church's ministries and normal operating expenses.

3. Why should contributions to the capital campaign be over and above regular tithes and offerings?

   The capital campaign is not to take away from the church's current ministry, nor is it to create a shortfall in the church's operating funds. Members must remain obedient in their regular tithes and offerings so they can remain in a right relationship with God. Capital funds are given from another, deeper, more sacrificial pocket. Capital gifts are short-term commitments that grow a believer's faith even further.

4. How long does a capital campaign usually take?

   One to three years

5. Why is it beneficial to use an outside consultant?

An outside consultant offers expertise, experience and credibility that ensures an effective capital campaign. A good consultant brings a proven, systematic plan that will result in a spiritual awakening of dormant gifts and talents, raise faith and raise the desired capital.

6. How does a church go about selecting the right consultant?

The consultant needs to match the church's profile and have a proven plan that is based on biblical principles. See the list of criteria in Part Three under "Selecting an Outside Consultant" for more details.

7. What costs should be considered when planning a capital campaign?

The cost of the consultant and the cost of implementing the campaign should be considered.

8. What is the role of preaching in a capital campaign?

Preaching is the greatest tool for stewardship transformation. Believers must hear from the pulpit what God wants them to know relative to money. Knowledge must be attained for faith to be raised. The best way to increase faith and knowledge is through anointed preaching.

9. What are some spiritual truths that should undergird any capital campaign?

Some spiritual truths that should undergird any capital campaign are:

- The expansion is not for the people, it is for God; and unless God builds it, it will not stand.
- Anything you do for God will meet with Satanic opposition.
- Building God's kingdom requires work. It is not easy. We must have a mind to work.
- Capital giving is a willing act of worship, privilege, inclusion and lavishness. It is an opportunity to lavishly pour our love out to God.
- The assurance that God will lead us in new endeavors is evidenced in what He has done for us in the past.
- If we let God lead our capital campaigns, it will revive us spiritually.

10. What are some of the common obstacles a church must overcome when implementing a capital campaign?

Some common obstacles are:

- Resistance to using an outside consultant
- Seeing the church as begging for money instead of building God's kingdom
- Believing that others will give so it is not necessary for me to give
- Members having spiritual cataracts instead of seeing with their spiritual eyes

# Lesson Four:
# Discovering the Joy of Giving

## Objective
The objective of this lesson is to usher the participant into the ultimate stewardship experience—the joy of giving.

## Study and Review

1. What is joy?

2. How do we derive true joy?

3. What is the joy of giving?

4. Why is tithing considered training wheels for discovering the joy of giving?

5. Stewardship is managing another's assets. How can Christians take stewardship to the next level?

6. What is the connection between our spiritual lives and money?

7. Why are we most like Jesus when we give?

8. Why is accepting that the earth is not our home critical to discovering the joy of giving?

9. How do we rob ourselves of joy?

10. Solomon said, *"Whoever loves money never has enough"* (Ecc. 5:10). In other words, the more we have, the more we want. How can we discover the joy of giving if we are always in want?

## Application

1. What must you do to personally experience the joy of giving? Pray for discernment. Ask God what you must do to be filled with the joy of giving.

2. If the Spirit of Christmas Past, Present and Future visited you, what things would he show you? What things in your past have influenced your giving? What things in your present would help you appreciate the goodness of God in your life? What future life would you see?

3. One minute after you die, what will you wish you had given away? What can you give now so that when you die, you can have the joy of knowing that you gave all you could to build God's kingdom? What's preventing you from giving it away while you are living?

4. What opportunities for giving is God giving you right now? What would happen if you obeyed His calling?

# Lesson Four:
# Discovering the Joy of Giving
# Study and Review Answer Sheet

1. What is joy?

   Joy is the happy state that results from knowing and serving God *(Holman Bible Dictionary)*.

2. How do we derive true joy?

   True joy comes from a right relationship with God.

3. What is the joy of giving?

   The joy of giving is the ultimate stewardship experience. You have discovered the joy of giving when your life's focus becomes pleasing God and fulfilling His purposes for His kingdom on earth.

4. Why is tithing considered training wheels for discovering the joy of giving?

   Tithing is the basic starting point for our giving. Once we have spiritually grown to the tithe, then we can begin to discover the joy of giving beyond that which is required.

5. Stewardship is managing another's assets. How can Christians take stewardship to the next level?

   The next level of stewardship is using all of our resources (money, time, talents, gifts and possessions) to build God's kingdom. We relinquish ownership of everything and adopt a lifestyle of stewardship.

6. What is the connection between our spiritual lives and money?

We cannot separate our spiritual lives from our money. Our behavior is our best evidence of what we really believe and who we really love. Obedient stewardship is evidence of our faithful belief in and love for God. We must repent of any sin in our lives so God can transform us into good stewards.

7. Why are we most like Jesus when we give?

Jesus gave. He gave His life so we could have salvation. His ministry on earth was filled with giving love, mercy, restoration and healing. Jesus is our example for giving. If we love Him, we will give more.

8. Why is accepting that the earth is not our home critical to discovering the joy of giving?

When we accept that the earth is not our home, then we will concern ourselves with storing our treasure in heaven instead of on earth, a place that we are just passing through.

9. How do we rob ourselves of joy?

When we don't give, we are no longer in a right relationship with God. We thereby rob ourselves of God who is the source of our joy.

10. Solomon said, *"Whoever loves money never has enough"* (Ecc. 5:10). In other words, the more we have, the more we want. How can we discover the joy of giving if we are always in want?

We can't. We cannot discover the joy of giving until we become satisfied that God has given us enough.

# Appendix

The materials in this section are provided as resources and examples to assist you in implementing God's Progressive Giving Plan. You may reproduce any materials within this section only.

# Index of Appendices

# Index of Appendices

# Stewardship Emphasis Planning Calendar

The following calendar assumes that November is Stewardship Emphasis Month and that the unified budget will be approved on the first Sunday in December.

| Month | Action/Event | Group Responsible |
|---|---|---|
| **Aug.** | Review the budget-making and budget-raising processes | Stewardship Ministry |
| | Establish a date for budget approval | Stewardship Ministry |
| | Select a theme | Stewardship Ministry |
| | Prepare budget guidelines | Budget & Accounting |
| | Assemble historical budget data for the church and auxiliaries | Budget & Accounting |
| | Project the next year's expenditures for each auxiliary based on current spending | Budget & Accounting |
| **Sept.** | Plan the Stewardship Leadership Workshop | Budget & Accounting |
| | Order commitment cards and envelopes | Education & Promotion |
| | Request auxiliary budgets from ministry leaders | Budget & Accounting |
| | Publish bulletin announcement for Stewardship Leadership Workshop (3rd & 4th Sunday) | Budget & Accounting |

**Appendix 1 (cont'd)**

| Month | Action/Event | Group Responsible |
|-------|-------------|-------------------|
| Oct. | Stewardship Leadership Workshop (1st Saturday) | Budget & Accounting |
| | Mail letters to previously committed members (1st Friday) | Education & Promotion |
| | Mail letters to noncommitted members (2nd Friday) | Education & Promotion |
| | Receive auxiliary budgets (due 3rd Saturday) | Budget & Accounting |
| | Review auxiliary budgets | Budget & Accounting |
| | Publish schedule of events for Stewardship Emphasis Month (3rd & 4th Sunday) | Education & Promotion |
| | Distribute Sunday School and Bible Study lessons to teachers (end of month) | Education & Promotion |
| Nov. | Present recommended unified budget (1st Saturday) | Budget & Accounting |
| | Acknowledgement Sunday (1st Sunday)<br>- Commitment cards in bulletins<br>- Testimony<br>- Report commitment results to pastor | Education & Promotion |
| | Financial Planning Workshop (2nd Saturday) | Education & Promotion |
| | Bible Study Lesson (Wednesday before 2nd Sunday) | Bible Study Teachers |
| | Prove the Tithe Sunday (2nd Sunday)<br>- Commitment cards in bulletins<br>- Testimony<br>- Report commitment results to pastor | Education & Promotion |

| Month | Action/Event | Group/Person Responsible |
|-------|-------------|--------------------------|
| **Nov.** | Sunday School Lesson (2nd Sunday) | Sunday School Teachers |
| | Ministry Expo (2nd Sunday) | Budget & Accounting |
| | Commitment Sunday (3rd Sunday)<br>- Commitment cards in bulletins<br>- Testimony<br>- Report commitment results to pastor | Education & Promotion |
| | Revise recommended unified budget to create proposed unified budget | Budget & Accounting |
| | Publish proposed unified budget in bulletin (3rd Sunday) | Budget & Accounting |
| | Victory Sunday (4th Sunday)<br>- Announce commitment results to congregation<br>- Commitment cards in bulletins<br>- Testimony<br>- Report final results to pastor | Education & Promotion |
| **Dec.** | Approve proposed unified budget (1st Sunday) | Budget & Accounting |
| | Thank you notice in bulletin (2nd Sunday) | Education & Promotion |
| | Move Up Sunday reminder in bulletin (3rd & 4th Sunday) | Education & Promotion |
| **Jan.** | Move Up Sunday reminder in bulletin (1st Sunday) | Education & Promotion |
| | Approved budget published in bulletin | Budget & Accounting |

**Appendix 2**

# Budget-Making Planning Checklist

| Item No. | Action | Person Responsible | Due Date |
|---|---|---|---|
| 1. | Prepare budget guidelines and worksheets. | | |
| 2. | Assemble historical budget data for the church and auxiliaries. | | |
| 3. | Project next year's expenditures for each auxiliary. | | |
| 4. | Plan Leadership Workshop. | | |
| 5. | Send letter to request auxiliary budgets. | | |
| 6. | Publish bulletin announcement for Leadership Workshop. | | |
| 7. | Conduct Leadership Workshop. | | |
| 8. | Receive all auxiliary budgets. | | |
| 9. | Review auxiliary budgets. | | |
| 10. | Create recommended unified budget. | | |
| 11. | Publish bulletin announcement for meeting to discuss recommended unified budget. | | |
| 12. | Present recommended unified budget. | | |
| 13. | Revise recommended unified budget to create proposed unified budget. | | |
| 14. | Coordinate Ministry Expo. | | |

# Budget-Making Planning Checklist

| Item No. | Action | Person Responsible | Due Date |
|---|---|---|---|
| 15. | Publish proposed unified budget. | | |
| 16. | Publish bulletin announcement for budget approval meeting. | | |
| 17. | Present proposed unified budget for approval. | | |
| 18. | Publish approved unified budget in bulletin. | | |

**Appendix 3**

# Budget-Raising Planning Checklist

| Item No. | Action | Person Responsible | Due Date |
|---|---|---|---|
| 1. | Design and order commitment cards. | | |
| 2. | Draft letters to committed and non-committed members for the pastor's approval and signature. | | |
| 3. | Mail letters to previously committed members. | | |
| 4. | Mail letters to noncommitted members. | | |
| 5. | Publish schedule of events for Stewardship Emphasis Month. | | |
| 6. | Select and distribute Sunday School and Bible Study lessons. | | |
| 7. | Enlist people to give testimonies on all four promotional Sundays. | | |
| 8. | Provide commitment cards to people who prepare the bulletins for worship. | | |
| 9. | Plan Financial Planning Workshop. | | |
| 10. | Conduct Financial Planning Workshop. | | |
| 11. | Report weekly commitment results to pastor. | | |
| 12. | Give commitment cards to Financial Secretary. | | |
| 13. | Publish thank you notice in bulletin. | | |
| 14. | Publish move up Sunday reminder in bulletin. | | |

# Stewardship Emphasis Schedule
## *GIVE: That All May Know*

**1st Saturday in November**
BUDGET PLANNING MEETING, (time & location)

**1st Sunday in November**
ACKNOWLEDGEMENT SUNDAY—*Acknowledge God as creator, owner, redeemer and sustainer.*

**Wednesday before 2nd Sunday in November**
STEWARDSHIP BIBLE STUDY LESSON

**2nd Saturday in November**
FINANCIAL PLANNING WORKSHOP—*Learn to apply biblical principles of money management to your personal finances.*
(time and location)

**2nd Sunday in November**
PROVE THE TITHE SUNDAY—*Let's practice Malachi 3:10 and prove God's faithfulness by giving a tithe (10%) of our weekly income.*

STEWARDSHIP SUNDAY SCHOOL LESSON

MINISTRY EXPO, (time and location)

**3rd Sunday in November**
COMMITMENT SUNDAY—*Make our written commitments.*

**4th Sunday in November**
VICTORY SUNDAY—*Celebrate God's victory in our giving.*

**1st Sunday in December**
BUDGET APPROVAL MEETING, (time and location)

**1st Sunday in January**
MOVE UP SUNDAY—*We begin fulfilling our new commitments.*

**Appendix 5**

# Request for Auxiliary Budgets

(Date)

To:        All Ministry Leaders

From:     Stewardship Ministry Chairperson

RE:       (Year) Budget Planning

It's budget preparation time! We are excited about the many opportunities for ministry God is giving us. With so many opportunities, it is important that we are good stewards in planning our expenditures. Please keep in mind that our expense budget cannot exceed 95% of our projected revenues for (year).

Historical financial information and budget worksheets are enclosed. Your line item responsibility is highlighted. The historical data reflects our actual expenditures in (previous year) and current expenditures through August (current year). We have also projected your expenditures at your ministry's current spending rate. Please review this information carefully and contact me if you have questions. Below is our budget planning schedule.

**Budget Planning Schedule** (with actual dates)

| | |
|---|---|
| Sept. | Distribute historical information and budget worksheets |
| Oct. | Stewardship Leadership Workshop |
| Oct. | Auxiliary budget requests due to Stewardship Ministry |
| Nov. | Budget Planning Meeting (for recommended budget) |
| Nov. | Ministry Expo |
| Nov. | Proposed budget distributed to congregation |
| Dec. | Budget approval |

# Stewardship Leadership Workshop
# Bulletin Announcement
### (3rd & 4th Sunday in September)

## Stewardship Leadership  Workshop
for
All Church Leaders, Associate Ministers, Deaconship, Trusteeship,
Stewardship, Sunday School Workers, Auxiliary Chairpersons,
Auxiliary Workers, Members

Please come to discuss the (next year) budget planning
process and guidelines.

(Date)
(Time)
(Location)

**Appendix 7**

# Stewardship Leadership Workshop Agenda

Prayer

Overview of Budget Process

(Next Year) Budget Guidelines

Completing Budget Worksheets

Stewardship Emphasis Schedule

Ministry Expo
    Displays
    Setup
    Cleanup

Prayer

# Commitment Card

---

### (Next Year) God's Progressive Giving Plan
### *"RE" COMMITMENT CARD*

Recognizing that God is creator and owner of all things, I AFFIRM THAT: Jesus Christ is the Lord of all things; I should use all things according to His purpose; I am happy to make the following commitment of my financial resources.

### (Please complete all blanks below.)

I am now giving __% of my income through my church.

I recommit to give __% of my income in (next year) through my church.

I plan to increase my commitment each year for the next five years by __%. (Example: ½%, 1%, 2%, etc.)

**Name (please print)** _____

**Signature**_____**Envelope #**_____

---

**NOTE:** The commitment card is 3½" x 5½" and printed on cardstock.

**Appendix 8 (cont'd)**

# Commitment Card

---

## (Next Year) God's Progressive Giving Plan
### *"FIRST-TIME" COMMITMENT CARD*

Recognizing that God is creator and owner of all things, I AFFIRM THAT: Jesus Christ is the Lord of all things; I should use all things according to His purpose; I am happy to make the following commitment of my financial resources.

### **(Please complete all blanks below.)**

I commit to give __% of my income in (next year) through my church.

I plan to increase my commitment each year for the next five years by __%. (Example: ½%, 1%, 2%, etc.)

**Name (please print)** _____

**Signature**_____**Envelope #_____

---

**NOTE:** Print "First-Time" card in a different color.

# Giving Growth Guide

| GIVING GROWTH GUIDE | | | | | | | | | | |
|---|---|---|---|---|---|---|---|---|---|---|
| Weekly Income | Percent of Income to be Given | | | | | | | | | |
| | 2% | 45 | 6% | 8% | 10% | 12% | 14% | 16% | 18% | 20% |
| $100 | 2.00 | 4.00 | 6.00 | 8.00 | 10.00 | 12.00 | 14.00 | 16.00 | 18.00 | 22.00 |
| 150 | 3.00 | 6.00 | 9.00 | 12.00 | 15.00 | 18.00 | 21.00 | 24.00 | 27.00 | 30.00 |
| 200 | 4.00 | 8.00 | 12.00 | 16.00 | 20.00 | 24.00 | 28.00 | 32.00 | 36.00 | 40.00 |
| 250 | 5.00 | 10.00 | 15.00 | 20.00 | 25.00 | 30.00 | 35.00 | 40.00 | 45.00 | 50.00 |
| 300 | 6.00 | 12.00 | 18.00 | 24.00 | 30.00 | 36.00 | 42.00 | 48.00 | 54.00 | 60.00 |
| 350 | 7.00 | 14.00 | 21.00 | 28.00 | 35.00 | 42.00 | 49.00 | 56.00 | 63.00 | 70.00 |
| 400 | 8.00 | 16.00 | 24.00 | 32.00 | 40.00 | 48.00 | 56.00 | 64.00 | 72.00 | 80.00 |
| 450 | 9.00 | 18.00 | 27.00 | 36.00 | 45.00 | 54.00 | 63.00 | 72.00 | 81.00 | 90.00 |
| 500 | 10.00 | 20.00 | 30.00 | 40.00 | 50.00 | 60.00 | 70.00 | 80.00 | 90.00 | 100.00 |
| 550 | 11.00 | 22.00 | 33.00 | 44.00 | 55.00 | 66.00 | 77.00 | 88.00 | 99.00 | 110.00 |
| 600 | 12.00 | 24.00 | 36.00 | 48.00 | 60.00 | 72.00 | 84.00 | 96.00 | 108.00 | 120.00 |
| 650 | 13.00 | 26.00 | 39.00 | 52.00 | 65.00 | 78.00 | 91.00 | 104.00 | 117.00 | 130.00 |
| 700 | 14.00 | 28.00 | 42.00 | 56.00 | 70.00 | 84.00 | 98.00 | 112.00 | 126.00 | 140.00 |
| 750 | 15.00 | 30.00 | 45.00 | 60.00 | 75.00 | 90.00 | 105.00 | 120.00 | 135.00 | 150.00 |
| 800 | 16.00 | 32.00 | 48.00 | 64.00 | 80.00 | 96.00 | 112.00 | 128.00 | 144.00 | 160.00 |
| 850 | 17.00 | 34.00 | 51.00 | 68.00 | 85.00 | 102.00 | 119.00 | 136.00 | 153.00 | 170.00 |

**NOTE:** The Giving Growth Guide is printed on the reverse side of both commitment cards. (See Appendix 8.)

**Appendix 10**

# Letter to Committed Members

(Date)


Dear Committed Member:

Our annual Stewardship Emphasis begins Sunday, (1st Sunday in November). Our theme this year is *"Give: That All May Know (3 John: 1–8)."* The early church depended on preachers, teachers, evangelists and missionaries traveling from place to place to spread the gospel. John encouraged believers to provide resources so these witnesses could continue their efforts for Christ. Through tithing we can share the gospel so that all people of the world may know the good news of salvation through Jesus Christ.

All of us are challenged to find greater levels of commitment in our spiritual lives and in our giving. God expects us to grow in our giving as we mature spiritually. Therefore, I am asking you to pray about your spiritual and financial gifts, and then to recommit to a purposeful giving plan. Please return the enclosed commitment card for (next year) before (1st Sunday in November) so we can use the number of early commitments as a testimony to encourage new members. Your commitment card from last year and a self-addressed return envelope are enclosed for your convenience. Thank you for continuing your effort to *"Give: That All May Know."*

Yours in Christ


Pastor's Signature

# Letter to Noncommitted Members

(Date)


Dear Member:

Each November we plan activities to challenge us to a deeper level of commitment in our spiritual lives and in our giving. These activities are not merely to raise funds, but to encourage us to grow in our understanding and commitment to Christ.

Our annual Stewardship Emphasis begins Sunday, (1st Sunday in November). Our theme this year is *"Give: That All May Know (3 John:1–8)."* The early church depended on preachers, teachers, evangelists and missionaries traveling from place to place to spread the gospel. John encouraged believers to provide resources so these witnesses could continue their efforts for Christ. Through tithing we can share the gospel so that all people of the world may know the good news of salvation through Jesus Christ.

I am asking all members to prayerfully consider their spiritual and financial gifts to the church in (next year), and to return the enclosed commitment card either by mail or during one of our worship services. You will be hearing more about Stewardship Emphasis. Please pray that we meet our goals.

Yours in Christ


Pastor's Signature

**Appendix 12**

# Commitment Tracking Form

Create electronic spreadsheets like the table below to track the number of commitments at each percentage level in half percent increments up to 20% on a year-to-year basis. Maintain separate sheets for "First-Time" and "Re" commitments.

| % | Acknowledge-ment Sunday | | Prove the Tithe Sunday | | Commitment Sunday | | Victory Sunday | | 5th Sunday | | .5 |
|---|---|---|---|---|---|---|---|---|---|---|---|
| | Year | Year | Year | Year | Year | Year | Year | Year | Year | Year | |
| .5 | | | | | | | | | | | 1.5 |
| 1 | | | | | | | | | | | 2 |
| 1.5 | | | | | | | | | | | 2.5 |
| 2 | | | | | | | | | | | 3 |
| 2.5 | | | | | | | | | | | 3.5 |
| 3 | | | | | | | | | | | 4 |
| 3.5 | | | | | | | | | | | 4.5 |
| 4 | | | | | | | | | | | 5 |
| 4.5 | | | | | | | | | | | 5.5 |
| 5 | | | | | | | | | | | 6 |
| 5.5 | | | | | | | | | | | 6.5 |
| 6 | | | | | | | | | | | 7 |
| 6.5 | | | | | | | | | | | 7.5 |
| 7 | | | | | | | | | | | 8 |
| 7.5 | | | | | | | | | | | 8.5 |
| 8 | | | | | | | | | | | 9 |
| 8.5 | | | | | | | | | | | 9.5 |
| 9 | | | | | | | | | | | 10 |
| 9.5 | | | | | | | | | | | 10.5 |
| 10 | | | | | | | | | | | 11 |
| 10.5 | | | | | | | | | | | 11.5 |
| 11 | | | | | | | | | | | 12 |
| Others | | | | | | | | | | | Others |
| Total | | | | | | | | | | | Total |

# Sample Use of Performance Data Bulletin Insert

## This is the Record

| Year | Families | Church Budget |
|------|----------|---------------|
| 1979 | | $30,694 |
| 1980 | | 56,000 |
| 1981 | | 68,376 |
| 1982 | | 112,136 |
| 1983 | | 133,682 |
| 1984 | | 180,218 |
| 1985 | | 213,787 |
| 1986 | | 230,000 |
| 1987 | 424 | 303,746 |
| 1988 | 564 | 450,000 |
| 1989 | 819 | 795,304 |
| 1990 | 1,074 | 988,370 |
| 1991 | 1,284 | 1,113,305 |
| 1992 | 1,443 | 1,442,509 |
| 1993 | 1,586 | 1,674,320 |
| 1994 | 1,743 | 1,725,000 |
| 1995 | 1,978 | 2,059,826 |
| 1996 | 2,293 | 2,232,318 |
| 1997 | 2,544 | 2,637,238 |
| 1998 | 2,431 | 2,214,625 |
| 1999 | 2,622 | 3,514,631 |
| 2000 | 2,734 | 4,100,000 |
| 2001 | 2,789 | 4,857,000 |
| 2002 | 2,856 | 4,900,000 |
| 2003 | 2,921 | 5,409,942 |

### This We Are Able

A. Number of resident church families      2921

B. Average family income data per 1995 county records      $38,189

C. Multiply Line A x Line B      $111,550,069

D. One tenth (a tithe) of Line C      $11,155,007

**Appendix 14**

# Budget Planning Meeting
# Bulletin Announcement

**(3rd & 4th Sunday in October)**

## (Next Year) Budget Planning Meeting

for

All Church Leaders, Associate Ministers, Deaconship, Trusteeship,
Stewardship, Sunday School Workers, Auxiliary Chairpersons,
Auxiliary Workers, Members

Please come to discuss the recommended unified budget for (next year).

(Date)
(Time)
(Location)

# Recommended Unified Budget

| Accounts | Budget Previous Year | YTD Actuals | Projected End of Year | Requested Amount | Recom'd Next Year |
|---|---|---|---|---|---|
| **INCOME** | | | | | |
| Unified Budget | | | | | |
| Capital Campaign | | | | | |
| Total Income | | | | | |
| **MINISTRIES** | | | | | |
| Stewardship | | | | | |
| Evangelism | | | | | |
| Christian Education | | | | | |
| Total Ministries | | | | | |
| **MISSIONS** | | | | | |
| Feed the Homeless | | | | | |
| Foreign Missionaries | | | | | |
| Total Missions | | | | | |
| **PERSONNEL** | | | | | |
| **UTILITIES** | | | | | |
| **Total Expenses** | | | | | |
| **Income over Expenses** | | | | | |

**Appendix 16**

# Financial Planning Workshop
# Bulletin Announcement

**(4th Sunday in October, 1st Sunday in November)**

## Financial Planning Workshop

Christian Money Management Makes $ense!
Join us to learn how to apply God's principles to your personal finances.

Topics will include:
Making the Most Out of Your Dollars
Dealing with Credit & Debt Reduction
Savings
Retirement
Developing a Family Budget
Estate Planning

(Date)
(Time)
(Location)

# Ministry Expo Participation Appeal

(Date)

To:          All Ministry Leaders

From:       Stewardship Ministry Chairperson

RE:          Ministry Expo

Each ministry is invited to participate in the Ministry Expo on Sunday, (date) at (time) immediately following the eleven o'clock worship service. As you know, this is "Prove the Tithe Sunday." We want the congregation to visually see how your ministry is using your allocated budget. This is an excellent opportunity to show and prove your ministry's accountability.

Please prepare a well thought out, tasteful display. Setup is scheduled for Saturday, (date) from (time). Contact the Facilities Management Staff by (date) to request tables, extension cords, chairs, etc. Your advance planning will be greatly appreciated. Also, please plan to assist with the cleanup after the expo.

Thank you for all that you do. Please contact me immediately if you have any questions.

**Appendix 18**

## Ministry Expo
## Bulletin Announcement
**(1st and 2nd Sunday in November)**

# MINISTRY EXPO

Come learn about our many ministries. See firsthand how your tithes and offerings are being used to build God's kingdom.

Displays, Information, Fun Refreshments, Free Gifts

Everyone is invited!

(Date)
(Time)
(Location)

# Budget Approval Meeting
# Bulletin Announcement
### (3rd & 4th Sunday in November)

# (Next Year) Budget Approval Meeting
(Date)
(Time)
(Location)

Please join us immediately following 11:00 a.m. worship as we discern God's will and ratify next year's budget.

**Appendix 20**

# Proposed Unified Budget

| Accounts | Budget Previous Year | YTD Actuals | Projected End of Year | Recom'd Next Year |
|---|---|---|---|---|
| **INCOME** | | | | |
| Unified Budget | | | | |
| Capital Campaign | | | | |
| Total Income | | | | |
| **MINISTRIES** | | | | |
| Stewardship | | | | |
| Evangelism | | | | |
| Christian Education | | | | |
| Total Ministries | | | | |
| **MISSIONS** | | | | |
| Feed the Homeless | | | | |
| Foreign Missionaries | | | | |
| Total Missions | | | | |
| **PERSONNEL** | | | | |
| **UTILITIES** | | | | |
| **Total Expenses** | | | | |
| **Income over Expenses** | | | | |

# Thank You Notice
# Bulletin Announcement
**(2nd Sunday in December)**

*Thank You*

Thanks to all who made commitments to give through our church by returning your (next year) commitment cards. Thank you for meeting the challenge of reaching for a deeper level of commitment in our spiritual lives and our giving. Your tithes and offerings will enable our church to increase its ministry and fulfill the purposes of God. Thank you for giving so that all may know Christ.

**Appendix 22**

## Move Up Sunday Reminder
## Bulletin Announcement

**(3rd & 4th Sunday in December, 1st Sunday in January)**

# Move Up Sunday

(Date)

# Monthly Budget Report
# Bulletin Insert

**(Every 1st Sunday)**

## Church Name

### Projected Income vs. Actual Income for (Year)
*"A goal untold is a defeatist attitude."*

### (Year) Projected Unified Budget $(Amount)

| Description | 1st Sun. | 2nd Sun. | 3rd Sun. | 4th Sun. | 5th Sun. | Weekly Avg. This Month | Weekly Avg. YTD | Total this Month | Total YTD |
|---|---|---|---|---|---|---|---|---|---|
| Total Needed Per Week $ (amount) | | | | | | | | | |
| Actual Received in (month) | | | | | | | | | |
| Total [deficit] or surplus | | | | | | | | | |

**Appendix 24**

# Stewardship Sunday School Lesson: Honor and Blessing in Giving

## by
## Charles W. Buffington

### Leader's Guide

As you study and prepare for this lesson, pray for God's fresh anointing to open the hearts and minds of your class members.

**I. Create Interest**

Consider a thought provoking way to lead into the lesson. It is very important to capture the class' interest and attention at the outset. Pray, asking God for inspiration and guidance in what to use for this purpose. Look for interesting current events or well-known historical events that support the key concepts of the lesson. Use personal experiences (testimony) that taught you the "lesson." When using personal testimony, create drama by telling just enough of the story to get everyone's interest, but save the punchline for later. Don't give away the end of the movie!

Another way of creating interest is by asking a series of open-ended questions that promote thought and discussion. Some examples that may be used with this lesson are:

* Why does God put so much emphasis on giving throughout the Bible?
* How do we give to receive honor?
* What are the results or benefits of obeying and honoring God?
* Why is it important for God's people to make and keep commitments (covenants)?

# Honor and Blessing in Giving: Leader's Guide

### II. Lesson Aim (Objective)
This lesson is to encourage class members to fully commit to God's plan to provide blessings of resources to church, community, family and individuals. God's plan is based on the concept of the tithe, the tenth that is given to honor Him.

### III. Background and Overview
Give an overview of the lesson emphasizing that through the study of this lesson, we will discover what God says about giving. Studying selected passages from both the Old and New Testaments, we will see what his expectations are and why giving is so fundamental to the Christian walk. Also, we will discover how God responds to our obedience in the area of giving.

### IV. Scripture Reading and Discussion
A. Honoring God by Righteously Giving (Genesis 4:1–11)
B. Obeying God in Giving (1 Kings 17:7–16, Matthew 6:33)
C. Believing God by Giving the Tithe (Malachi 3:8–12, Luke 6:38)

### V. Discussion Questions
A. Honoring God by Righteously Giving (Genesis 4:1–11)
1. Why did Cain and Abel bring an offering to God?
   Answer: To worship and thank God.
2. From where did their offering come?
   Answer: From their labor as a product of the time and talent that God gave them to pursue their vocations. Time + Talent = Treasure

**Appendix 24 (cont'd)**

# Honor and Blessing in Giving: Leader's Guide

### V. Discussion Questions (cont'd)

A. Honoring God by Righteously Giving (Genesis 4:1–11)

  3. Why did God accept Abel's offering and reject Cain's?

  4. What were the consequences of Cain's failure to worship God righteously?

  5. What makes our tithes and offerings acceptable to God?

B. Obeying God in Giving (1 Kings 17:7–16, Matthew 6:33)

  1. What could the widow have cited as reasons for *not* giving?

  2. What did the prophet identify as a barrier that she had overcome in order to give?
    Answer: Fear (Discuss verse 13.)

  3. What barriers must we overcome to fully commit to God's economy?
    Answer: Fear (Explain that fear and faith are mutually exclusive. Fear and faith cannot exist in the same space because one is light (faith) and one is darkness (fear).

  4. How did this widow's experience reflect the values found in Matthew 6:33?

C. Believing God by Giving the Tithe (Malachi 3:8–12, Luke 6:38)

  1. Before discussing these verses, give a brief background on the book of Malachi. Make the following points:

    a. Malachi is the last book of the Old Testament

    b. Malachi is followed by 400 years of silence wherein God does not send a prophetic word. Therefore, we must listen intently to these final words.

# Honor and Blessing in Giving: Leader's Guide

    C. Believing God by Giving the Tithe (Malachi 3:8–12, Luke 6:38)
        1. c. This book is admonishing Israel for their ingratitude and carelessness in their worship. This ties back to the first part of the lesson in Genesis 4.
        2. Discussion questions
            a. Why is not paying the tithe robbing God?
            Answer: The tenth belongs to God whether we give it or not.
            b. What is the challenge that God presents in these verses?
            c. What does God promise will result from our obedience in the tithe?
            Answer: Overflowing blessings, super abundance; rebuke the devourer; our fruit will reach ripeness and maturity; great witness in the world, all nations shall call you blessed; you shall be a delightful land because God said so!

## VI. Practical Application of the Word

    A. Invite personal testimonies on blessings received by righteous giving.
    B. Submit your commitment card and encourage others to do likewise.
    C. Challenge the class to reflect on the lesson and share what they learned with family and friends.

## VII. Outreach/Benevolence

## VIII. Closing Prayer

**Appendix 24 (cont'd)**

# Stewardship Sunday School Lesson:
# Honor and Blessing in Giving
### by
### Charles W. Buffington
### Learner's Guide

## Introduction

Once a year in November, we emphasize stewardship. This is the time of year when we teach and promote the spiritual values inherent in righteous giving and management of our resources, time, talent and treasure. This year's study focuses on the call to honor God through our giving and the benefits of obedience to His Word.

## Focal Passages

Genesis 4:1–11          Malachi 3:8-12

1 Kings 17:7–16          Luke 6:38

Matthew 6:33

## Central Bible Truth

We are called to honor God by obeying Him in all things including His statutes on tithes and offerings. He rewards our obedience with overflowing blessings.

## Lesson Aim

This lesson is to encourage class members to consider God's plan for prosperity and make a commitment to trust and obey Him by righteously giving.

# Honor and Blessing in Giving: Learner's Guide

**Scripture Lessons**
**Honoring God by Righteously Giving (Genesis 4:1–11)**
This lesson illustrates the imperative to worship God by offering the first and best products of the time and talent that He has given each of us.

**Obeying God's Word in Giving (1 Kings 17:7–16, Matthew 6:33)**
This lesson shows the relationship between obedience and God's continuing provision. The widow's faith in believing and acting in accordance with the Word of God turned on the faucet through which God's limitless blessings flow.

**Believing God by Giving the Tithe (Malachi 3:8–12, Luke 6:38)**
In this final part of the lesson, God is speaking directly to us through the prophet Malachi. He asserts that a robbery has occurred in that what is rightfully His has been withheld. He has been robbed in worship. He then asks that we try Him and allow Him to prove His ability to keep His promise of overflowing blessings.

**Bible Truths**
1. Righteous giving, tithes and offerings are an act of worship because it honors God.
2. God calls believers to give Him first priority in all things.
3. God's Word/promise provides a guarantee of blessings resulting from obedience in righteous giving.
4. We must commit to obey God in everything by faith.

**Appendix 24 (cont'd)**

# Honor and Blessing in Giving: Learner's Guide

**Practical Application of the Word**
1. Obey God by doing what He instructs you to do in His Word.
2. Pray for God's direction in what He would have you to commit in addition to what is explicit in His Word.
3. Develop the practice of writing your commitments and goals.
4. Make preparation to receive your overflowing blessings.

**Outreach/Benevolence**

**Closing Prayer**
Pray for the full implementation of God's economic plan in your life, your family and the church. Give God the **adoration** and praise that He is so worthy of because of who He is. **Confess** that we haven't done all that we ought do in the area of stewardship. Thank Him for the time, talent and treasure that He continues to invest with us. Make **supplication** for the faith to obey Him in what He has called us to do.

# Stewardship Sunday School Lesson: Excellence in Worship

**by**
**Charles W. Buffington**

## Leader's Guide

As you study and prepare for this lesson, pray for God's fresh anointing to open the hearts and minds of your class members.

**I. Create Interest**

Consider a thought provoking way to lead into the lesson. It is very important to capture the class' interest and attention at the outset. Pray, asking God for inspiration and guidance in what to use for this purpose. Look for interesting current events or well-known historical events that support the key concepts of the lesson. Use personal experiences (testimony) that taught you the "lesson." When using personal testimony, create drama by telling just enough of the story to get everyone's interest, but save the punchline for later. Don't give away the end of the movie!

Another way of creating interest is by asking a series open-ended questions that promote thought and discussion. Some examples that may be used with this lesson are:

- Why does God put so much emphasis on giving throughout the Bible?
- How do we give to receive honor?
- What are the results or benefits of obeying and honoring God?
- Why is it important for God's people to make and keep commitments (covenants)?

**Appendix 25 (cont'd)**

# Excellence in Worship: Leader's Guide

## II. Lesson Aim (Objective)

This lesson is to encourage class members to make a personal, written commitment to obey God in providing financial support for the church through tithes and offerings. This lesson points out the obligations and blessings of biblically correct giving.

## III. Background and Overview

Give an overview of the lesson emphasizing that we will discover through the study of this lesson, how God views the imperative of scriptural giving. Studying selected passages from both the Old and New Testaments, we will see what his expectations are and why giving is so fundamental to the Christian walk. Also, we will discover how God responds to our obedience in the area of giving.

## IV. Scripture Reading and Discussion

A. Worshiping God with the Tithe (Genesis 28:10–22, Deuteronomy 12:4–7, Malachi 3:6–12)

The passages of scripture should be read and interpreted as a single unit to give the class background in the tithe as an integral part of worship. Jacob's vow of the tithe after witnessing a glimpse of heaven is an act of worship (Gen. 28:10–20). Moses giving the children of Israel final instructions on proper worship shows the significance that God attaches to the tithe (Deut. 12:4–7). The book of Malachi in rebuking the people for their neglect in worship points to the fact that they rob God by withholding His tithe. Taken together, these scriptures paint a clear and vivid picture of how God views the tithe in relation to worship.

# Honor and Blessing in Giving: Leader's Guide

    B.  Obeying God in Giving (1 Kings 17:7–16, Matthew 6:33)
This part of the lesson, taken from the New Testament, points out the great privilege and benefit that flows from the true worship of generous giving. Paul shows how the Macedonian churches exceeded his expectations in their zeal to give. They gave themselves first to the Lord. This is a great picture of sacrificial giving (2 Cor. 8:1–5). The seventh verse is the focal point just as we excel in other aspects of the Christian walk, we ought to excel in giving also. (2 Cor. 8:7). The ninth chapter of 2 Corinthians is a challenge to the church to live up to its reputation and commitment to giving. It is particularly important that we view this from the perspective of how God has blessed our church. The last part of this scripture highlights the glorious benefits of generous giving.

## V. Discussion Questions
    A.  Worshiping God with the Tithe
Genesis 28:10–22
      1.  How did Jacob respond to getting a preview of heaven?
Answer: He worshiped God!
      2.  How did he characterize the place?
Answer: "This is none other than the house of God; this is the gate of heaven."
      3.  What is the connection between the "house of God" and the tithe?
Answer: The tithe is a part of worship in the house of God.

**Appendix 25 (cont'd)**

# Excellence in Worship: Leader's Guide

**V. Discussion Questions (cont'd)**

B. Worshiping God with the Tithe
Deuteronomy 12:4–7
1. What is the connection between the tithe and the place of worship?
Answer: God chose the church as the place where He is to be worshiped with the tithe. This answers the question about whether or not giving to secular charities fulfills the requirement to tithe. It does not!
2. What promises can we draw from this passage?
Answer: The presence of the Lord and His blessings!

Malachi 3:6–12
1. Why is Jacob mentioned here after so many years have passed?
Answer: God is a promisekeeper. He promised to keep Israel (Jacob).
2. How do we return to God?
Answer: We stop the robbery!
3. How does God invite us to test Him?
Answer: Try tithing!

C. The Blessings of Sacrificial Giving
2 Corinthians 8:1–5,7
1. What was the attitude of the Macedonians toward giving to the ministry?
Answer: They were eager to give to the ministry, even beyond their means!

# Excellence in Worship: Leader's Guide

### V. Discussion Questions (cont'd)
    C. The Blessings of Sacrificial Giving
        2 Corinthians 8:1–5,7 (cont'd)
        2. How could you describe one who excels in the grace of giving?
          Answer: Glad, even eager to give; makes a sacrifice to honor God.

        2 Corinthians 9:1–4, 6–8
        1. What is our responsibility to encourage tithing?
          Answer: We must commit ourselves first, and then we should share our faith in tithing with others so that they may also enjoy the blessings of pleasing God.

### VI. Practical Application of the Word
    A. Invite personal testimonies on blessings received by righteous giving.
    B. Submit your commitment card and encourage the class members to do likewise.
    C. Challenge the class to reflect on the lesson and share what they learned with family and friends.

### VII. Outreach/Benevolence

### VIII. Closing Prayer

**Appendix 25 (cont'd)**

# Stewardship Sunday School Lesson: Excellence in Worship

### by
### Charles W. Buffington

### Learner's Guide

## Memory Verse

"But as you excel in everything—in faith, in speech, in knowledge, in complete earnestness and in your love for us—see that you also excel in this grace of giving" (2 Cor. 8:7 NIV).

## Central Bible Truth

God has ordained tithes and offerings as the means by which his church and its ministries are to be supported. God loves it when His people worship Him with excellence in giving.

## Lesson Aim

This lesson is to encourage class members to make a commitment to worship God in an excellent way.

I.  **Introduction: Background and Overview**

II. **Scripture Reading and Discussion**
    A.  **Worshiping God with the Tithe**
        1.  Jacob's Worship (Genesis 28:10–22)
        2.  Instructions on Worship (Deuteronomy 12:4–7)
        3.  Righteous Worship (Malachi 3:6–12)
    B.  **The Blessings of Sacrificial Giving**
        1.  Sacrificial Giving (2 Corinthians 8:1–5,7)
        2.  Excellent Example (2 Corinthians 9:1–4, 6–8)

# Excellence in Worship: Learner's Guide

### III. Practical Application of the Word
A. Based on today's lesson, what is God's standard and expectation for our giving as a part of worship?
B. How has this lesson inspired you in committing to this year's "God's Progressive Giving Plan"?
C. How can we be helpful in encouraging others to join us in truly worshiping God in an excellent way?
D. What are the promises of God to those who by faith obey Him in the grace of giving?

### IV. Outreach/Benevolence

### V. Closing Prayer

**Appendix 26**

# MONEY OVER MATTERS
**by**
**Wanda S. Wynn**

*Scene: Conversation between two neighbors who meet at their mail boxes and just happen to be members of the same church.*

Member #1 - Current Giver, Future Tither
Member #2 - Faithful Tither

Member #1: I sure hope your mail is more exciting than mine. All I ever get is a bunch of special requests.

Member #2: Special requests?

Member #1: Yep. Bill collectors, *requesting* me to come or call to make a special payment.

Member #2: Well those *bills* are indicative of the things you love the most. Where your money is so lies your heart also.

Member #1: I've heard that rhetoric before *(brushing neighbor off)*, but these bills are about survival. *(Shuffles through mail then holds up a card.)* Did you get one of these commitment cards from the church in your mail?

Member #2: Sure did, and I completed mine and turned it back in the very first Sunday they issued them in church.

Member #1: Well, I'm thinking about this thing and whether or not I'm going to buy into it. I mean, I made a *commitment* to **Jesus**, but I still don't know what that has to do with giving your money to the church.

Member #2: Then you will enjoy the sermons this month on stewardship. Pastor will teach us about giving according to God's Word.

Member #1: He's teaching that for a whole month? I always figured that he gave those sermons when the church needed a new roof or building fund or something. I usually don't go on those Sunday's. I don't want to hear about asking for money.

Member #2: So-o-o-o you don't give?

Member #1: Well, I give. But...

Member #2: But what? Are you one of those who give whatever is in your purse on Sunday morning...

Member #1: ...Minus whatever I need for Sunday brunch after church.

Member #2: Oh, I feel sorry for you.

**Appendix 26 (cont'd)**

Member #1: You do. Why?

Member #2: You're missing out on half the fun. You are missing the joy of giving.

Member #1: Fun? You think giving away your money is fun!

Member #2: Listen, are you sure you are a Christian? Because giving doesn't make sense to the **NONbelievers**. A Christian who isn't giving is kind of a contradiction in terms.

Member #1: I'm sorry, I don't understand what you mean, what is it that you are trying to say?

Member #2: Oh, how do I put this? I want to be careful because I don't want to offend you.

Member #1: Offend *me*? How could you offend me?

Member #2: Well, some people claim that they are Christians because they go to church or because their parents were Christians, but they have no **real** commitment to Jesus Christ.

Member #1: Well, I *am* a committed Christian. I go to church on Sunday, I say grace before my meals and I know Jesus is the Son of God, but I guess I missed the part of the sermon on giving that talked about fun.

Member #2: In the Old Testament, the Book of Malachi prom-ises that your storehouses won't be able to contain all your blessings when you start trusting the Lord with your money.

Member #1: You don't really believe that, do you?

Member #2: Believe it? Not only do believe it, I live it! I can't begin to tell you how God has blessed me. Once you start giving regularly and sacrificially for awhile, you soon realize that it is all God's money anyway.

Member #1: You sound like those people on that Capital Campaign Committee. I suppose you are on board with that too.

Member #2: As a matter of fact I am.

Member #1: How can you afford that? You must have a whole lot more money than I do. Like I said, *(holding and waving the bills)* these bills are about sur-vi-ving. And whenever I can, I do splurge on myself and buy things I like and enjoy. Am I not supposed to have one dime of my money for me? What about *my* needs?

Member #2: God's promise is to meet all of your NEEDS—not all your greeds. You can't measure by how much somebody else is giving.

**Appendix 26 (cont'd)**

Member #1: Look, my company just announced last week that they were laying off 500 people soon. I don't know if I will even have a job next year not to mention pledging a large amount of money over the next three years! And besides…What does the church do with all that money anyway?

Member #2: First of all the pledge is all about equal sacrifice, *not* equal gifts. And most importantly, tithing is not about money nor is it about what the church does with it. It is about **trust**.

Member #1: *Trust.* You lost me there.

Member #2: If you will trust God with your money, you will trust him with every aspect of your life. And God promised that he will reveal himself to those who trust him. See trusting God means you don't worry about layoffs and downsizing, 401Ks and the condition of the stock market tomorrow. You don't even worry about tomorrow because you know *"Who"* holds tomorrow.

Member #1: Well, I'm a relatively new Christian, and I don't have a lot of confidence in the promises of God, yet. So, I *have* to worry about what **I** do with my money and how far I can make it go.

Member #2: Well, let me share my experiences with you. Those who trust the Lord **most** with their money are those who worry **least** about money.

Member #1: That's interesting. I worry about money a lot. That's why I didn't fill out this commitment card. I don't know if I can commit.

Member #2: Then start giving for the peace of mind if nothing else.

Member #1: Somehow I can't see the *connection* between giving your money away and getting peace of mind.

Member #2: The connection is the **FAITH** factor.

Member #1: Faith?

Member #2: Faith. That is correct. Tithing is nothing more than a demonstration of your faith that God will help you live on 90 percent of your income. It's okay *(convincingly)*. Just *try* God. If **HE** gave his life for your eternal security, don't you think **HE** is worth risking a little money for?

Member #1: Alright. Go ahead and put me down for 10 percent. I guess I'll fill out this card after all.

Member #2: So, you're going to start tithing?

**Appendix 26 (cont'd)**

Member #1: Yes, *(breathing deeply)*. What have I done?

Member #2: You have decided to trust God. Now…*(comes closer to Member #1)*. This only works if you're smiling.

Member #1: Smiling?

Member #2: Yes smiling, because God loves a cheerful giver.

**THE END**

# Other Resources by George O. McCalep, Jr., Ph.D.
## *Committed to Doing Church God's Way*

# ORDER FORM

| QTY | ITEM | EACH | TOTAL |
|---|---|---|---|
| | Faithful Over a Few Things | 19.95 | |
| | Faithful Over a Few Things—Study Guide | 9.95 | |
| | Faithful Over a Few Things—Audio Version | 14.95 | |
| | Faithful Over a Few Things—Resource Kit | 189.95 | |
| | Breaking the Huddle | 14.95 | |
| | Breaking the Huddle—Sermonic Audiocassette | 10.00 | |
| | Growing Up to the Head | 19.95 | |
| | Growing Up to the Head—Leader's Guide | 10.95 | |
| | Growing Up to the Head—Participant's Guide | 10.95 | |
| | Stir Up the Gifts | 24.95 | |
| | Stir Up the Gifts—Leader's Guide | 10.95 | |
| | Stir Up the Gifts—Workbook & Study Guide | 10.95 | |
| | Stir Up the Gifts—Sermonic Audio Series | 19.95 | |
| | Praising the Hell Out of Yourself | 19.95 | |
| | Praising the Hell Out of Yourself—Workbook | 14.95 | |
| | Praising the Hell Out of Yourself—CD | 14.95 | |
| | Praising the Hell Out of Yourself—T-Shirt (L, XL, XXL, XXXL) | 10.00 | |
| | Sin in the House | 19.95 | |
| | How to Be Blessed | 19.95 | |
| | "Jabez's Prayer"—Sermonic Audio Series | 19.95 | |
| | A Good Black Samaritan | 3.95 | |
| | Messages of Victory for God's Church in the New Millennium—Sermonic Audio Series | 19.95 | |
| | Tough Enough: Trials on Every Hand by Sadie T. McCalep, Ph.D. | 20.00 | |
| | Fulfillment Hour by Jackie S. Henderson & Joan W. Johnson | 24.95 | |
| | Faith Raising vs. Money Raising | 24.95 | |
| | Subtotal | | |

# Order by phone, fax, mail or online

**Orman Press**
**4200 Sandy Lake Drive**
**Lithonia, GA  30038**
**Phone: 770-808-0999**
**Fax: 770-808-1955**

**www.ormanpress.com**

| ITEM | AMOUNT |
|---|---|
| Subtotal | |
| Postage & Handling (Call for Shipping Charges) | |
| C.O.D. (Add $6 plus Postage & Handling) | |
| **Total** | |

Date_____Name_____

Address_____Apt./Unit_____

City_____State_____Zip_____

Credit Card #_____Exp. Date_____

# Visit our web site @ www.ormanpress.com
# Your one-stop store for Christian resources

Pastor and Sister McCalep are available to conduct
workshops and seminars on all of these resources.
Call 404-486-6740 for scheduling information.

# THE AUTHOR'S COLLECTION

God has given me a burning passion for biblically based kingdom building and spiritual growth. Through His Spirit, I have discerned and recorded in my books discipleship principles related to church growth, evangelism, personal spiritual development, praise and worship. I recommend the following titles to those who are serious about *doing church God's way*.

## Church Growth and Kingdom Building

*Faithful Over a Few Things: Seven Critical Church Growth Principles* bridges the gap between theory and practice. It offers seven principles that when faithfully implemented will cause your church to grow. The book is available in print and audio versions. A study guide and resource kit are also available. The resource kit contains a workbook, transparencies and a videotape.

*Sin in the House: Ten Crucial Church Problems with Cleansing Solutions* examines problems that hinder growth and offers proven solutions. This book addresses the question of why you and your church are not growing.

*Fulfillment Hour: Fulfilling God's Purposes for the Church Through the Sunday School Hour* by Jackie S. Henderson and Joan W. Johnson presents a nontraditional Sunday School model that fulfills all of the purposes and mission of the church through a systematic, balanced and creative approach within the context of an hour. *Fulfillment Hour* explains the concept, process and procedures of the model in detail. The model can be applied by any denomination and church.

## Evangelism

*Breaking the Huddle* contains twelve messages that deal with the central theme of fulfilling Jesus' purpose of seeking and saving the lost (Luke 19:10). Like a football team, the church must break the huddle, that is, leave the comfort of the sanctuary and obediently go out among the unsaved to share the Gospel.

## Personal Spiritual Development

*Growing Up to the Head: Ten Essentials to Becoming a Better Christian* challenges the reader to mature spiritually by growing up to the fullness of Christ. The study is based on the book of Ephesians. The book uniquely relates personal spiritual growth to numerical congregational growth. A new participant's guide and leader's guide are now available.

*Stir Up the Gifts: Empowering Believers for Victorious Living and Ministry Tasks* is a complete, practical guide on spiritual gifts that is applicable for any denomination. The book is based on 2 Timothy 1:6 where Paul tells us to stir up the gift and bring the fire to a flame. Study of this book will fire you up and revolutionize the ministries in your church. A leader's guide and study guide are available.

*How to Be Blessed: Finding Favor with God and Man* is a biblical guide to being blessed according to God's Word. It is based on the truth that God promises to bless His obedient children. This book will protect you from finding out too late about all the blessings that were yours, but you never received.

## Praise and Worship

Although the title is colorful, *Praising the Hell Out of Yourself* is a beneficial discipleship approach to praise and worship. It offers praise as an antidote for evil and provides the "how, why and when" of entering into His presence. A workbook, CD and T-shirt are available.

## Inspiration

My wife's autobiography, ***Tough Enough: Trials on Every Hand*** describes how God transformed a shy, reserved, country girl from Alabama into a bold, self-assured, yet humble helpmeet to her husband and spokesperson for the Lord. Truly, you will be encouraged by her testimony of faith.

## Black History

***A Good Black Samaritan*** teaches biblical Black history—specifically how Jesus used people of color to teach the world what is good.